DAY TRIPS®
FROM MEMPHIS

Help Us Keep This Guide Up to Date

Every effort has been made by the authors and editors to make this guide as accurate and useful as possible. However, many things can change after a guide is published—establishments close, phone numbers change, facilities come under new management, etc.

We would love to hear from you concerning your experiences with this guide and how you feel it could be improved and kept up to date. While we may not be able to respond to all comments and suggestions, we'll take them to heart and we'll also make certain to share them with the authors. Please send your comments and suggestions to the following address:

The Globe Pequot Press
Reader Response/Editorial Department
P.O. Box 480
Guilford, CT 06437

Or you may e-mail us at:

editorial@globe-pequot.com

Thanks for your input, and happy travels!

Day Trips® Series

GETAWAYS LESS THAN TWO HOURS AWAY

DAY TRIPS®
FROM MEMPHIS

by

Rebecca Finlayson and Sally Sprott Pace

The Globe Pequot Press

GUILFORD, CONNECTICUT

Cover image: DubeStudio
Maps: William L. Nelson Cartography & Graphics

ISBN: 0-7627-1029-2
ISSN 1537-0534

Manufactured in the United States of America
First Edition/First Printing

 For Graham, the little explorer,
For Marshall, the lost traveler,
and
For Ashley, the constant compass

CONTENTS

ARKANSAS

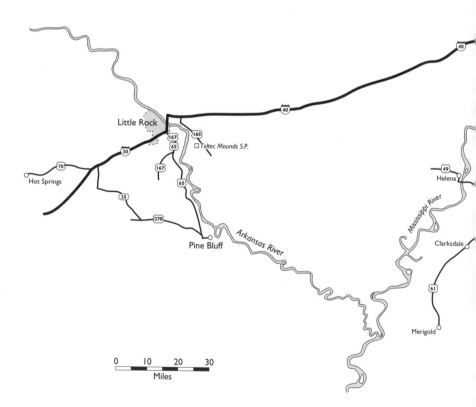

Jonesboro

63

40

Little Rock

167
165
65
□ Toltec Mounds S.P.

30

167

65

70

Hot Springs

49
Helena

35

270

Mississippi River

Pine Bluff

Arkansas River

Clarksdale

61

Merigold

0   10   20   30
Miles

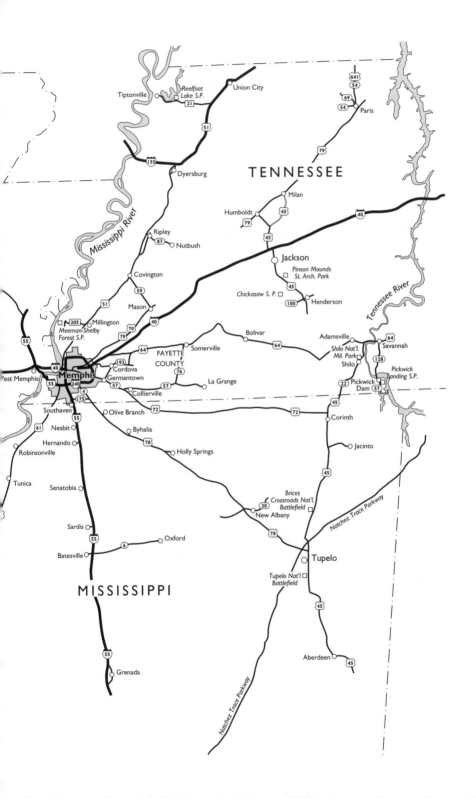

PREFACE

Memphis is located on the great Mississippi River at the intersection of three great states—Tennessee, Arkansas, and Mississippi—making this city a convenient center from which to travel. Going west, you'll hit Arkansas, former home of the Clintons; south, you'll enter Mississippi, steeped in Civil War history; north and east you'll relish the familiar territory of the western Tennessee flatlands. This geographic niche offers day trippers the chance to see three different states and a varied cultural terrain.

Whether you decide to take a ferry ride, explore outer space, camp lakeside, sing the blues, taste wine, enjoy an outdoor concert, eat a fried pork chop, tour an antebellum home, watch a Civil War film, hunt quail, hike through Native American mounds, sample a slug-burger, take a hot springs bath, or learn about Elvis's humble beginnings, you'll never have to drive more than an hour or two.

Memphis's own claims to fame are, of course, barbecue and music. For the last twenty years or so, it's been home to the international barbecue festival. And for more than fifty years, Memphis has been a music hotspot—both Elvis and the blues gained national recognition by way of Rock and Roll and Beale Street. Though you'll find that barbecue is a popular cuisine throughout the Midsouth and that the blues is a cultural mainstay in southern Arkansas and the Mississippi Delta, what makes this region most noteworthy is its Civil War history. Tennessee, in particular, has more Civil War sites than any other state except Virginia. And several major battles—the battles of Tupelo and Shiloh, for example—were staged in Mississippi.

Ultimately no matter which direction you decide to drive, you'll stumble upon something worth the trip. Midsoutherners throughout the area are sure to welcome you with a home-cooked meal, a warm smile, and an interesting story about days gone by.

TRAVEL TIPS

Road Maps

Although stumbling off the beaten path and onto a charming back-country road can be exciting and adventurous, you don't want to get lost. The maps provided in this book are accurate but not very detailed. So a road map of the state or region in which you're traveling is a good idea. You may also be interested in driving an alternate route to your day-trip destination. You can get a good road map at most bookstores and service stations or from automobile associations such as AAA. State departments of transportation can also mail you state and regional maps. In addition, the Internet has a wide selection of map Web sites—try www.mapquest.com—which can even provide you with driving directions should you decide to travel a different route.

For more information, contact the **Tennessee Department of Transportation** at (615) 741-2195 or (615) 741-3500; the **Arkansas State Highway and Transportation Department** at (501) 569-2444; or the **Mississippi Department of Transportation** at (601) 359-7045.

Follow the Rules of the Road

Because Memphis is nestled at the meeting point of Tennessee, Mississippi, and Arkansas, you'll be traveling the roads of three different states, and road rules vary among them. Generally speaking, interstate speed limits are 65 to 70 miles per hour; state and county roads allow you to go 45 to 55 miles per hour. In 2001 Tennessee passed a law requiring drivers and passengers to wear their seat belts, so buckle up. Families traveling together should also remember to keep children of less than forty pounds in a child-safety seat at all times while driving.

For information about highway construction, closed roads, and other traffic issues, contact the following departments of transportation: the **Tennessee Department of Transportation** at www.tdot.state.tn.us/ or (615) 741-2848; the **Mississippi Department of Transportation** at www.mdot.state.ms.us/ or (601) 359-7001; or the **Arkansas State Highway and Transportation Department** at www.ahtd.state.ar.us/ or (501) 569-2000.

Fall Foliage

If you're heading out for a day trip between mid-September and mid-November, consider a destination that will offer you the best chance to see the Midsouth's fall foliage. Call (800) 225-TRIP to find out where the peak colors are. You can also telephone Tennessee's **Fall Color Hotline,** which gives weekly updated and prerecorded information about where to see the changing leaves as well as what seasonal events are planned; call (800) 697-4200.

Call Ahead

If you've got your heart set on a particular restaurant or inn, it would be wise to call ahead to confirm hours of operation and availability. Also, many of the day trips around Memphis take you to small towns, so every once in a while a restaurant may be closed for the season (allowing the owner to take a much-needed vacation). All important telephone numbers are provided in this guide.

Watch Out for Animals

Because many of the day trips in this book take you through wooded and undeveloped areas, you'll want to be on the lookout for wild animals (deer, raccoons, and other wildlife). Also, many of the state and county roads taking you to your destination meander through rural areas, where livestock may pose a driving hazard. Some of these roads have warning signs alerting you to the presence of loose animals, but many don't; just stay aware.

Sleeping Away from Home

Although the destinations in this book can all be visited in just one day, you may want to spend the night and really soak up the area, hitting all the tourist spots and indulging in your escape from Memphis. Some of the day trips take you to places with divine hotels or cozy B&Bs, too, where spending the night is actually the best attraction. And let's face it, you may just be too tired to make the drive home.

If you do decide to stay for the night, you'll be able to find lodging for nearly every day trip in this book. There is a variety of options—from grand hotels, like the Arlington in Hot Springs, to charming bed-and-breakfasts, like the Edwardian Inn in Helena. In addition, a few destinations offer more standard road hotel-motel lodging, such as the Holiday Inn Express in New Albany.

For the most part, the lodging provided in this guide ranges in price from $50 to $100, with the B&Bs being on the higher end. There are also a few upper-crust hotels like the Little Rock Peabody where visitors wanting to splurge can hunker down for the night. For the B&Bs and the more luxurious hotels, it's a good idea to call ahead for reservations.

The **Tennessee Bed & Breakfast Innkeepers Association** can provide you with brochures and information about its members. Write the association at P.O. Box 120428, Nashville, TN 37212, or call (800) 820-8144. You also might want to contact the **Bed & Breakfast About Tennessee** at (800) 458-2421, where booking agents can help you with reservations. For Mississippi B&Bs, write to the **Mississippi Bed and Breakfast Association** at 2430 Drummond Street, Vicksburg, MS 39180, or call (601) 638-8893. And for Arkansas B&Bs, write the **Arkansas Bed and Breakfast Association** at P.O. Box 250261, Little Rock, AR 72225-0261, or e-mail bbaa@bbonline.com. In addition, all chambers of commerce and visitor bureaus listed in the back of this book under Regional Information will be happy to send you complete listings of lodging in their areas.

USING THIS TRAVEL GUIDE

Highway designations: Federal highways are designated US. State routes are indicated by TN for Tennessee, MS for Mississippi, and AR for Arkansas.

Hours: Hours of operation have generally been omitted because they are subject to frequent change. Instead, addresses and phone numbers are provided so that you can obtain the most up-to-date information.

Restaurants: Restaurant prices are designated as $$$ (expensive; $15 and over for an entree), $$ (moderate; $5–$15), and $ (inexpensive; $5 and under).

Accommodations: Room prices are designated as $$$ (expensive; over $100 for a standard room), $$ (moderate; $50–100), and $ (inexpensive; under $50).

Credit cards: The symbol □ denotes that credit cards are accepted.

The prices and rates listed in this guidebook were confirmed at press time. We recommend, however, that you call establishments before traveling to obtain current information.

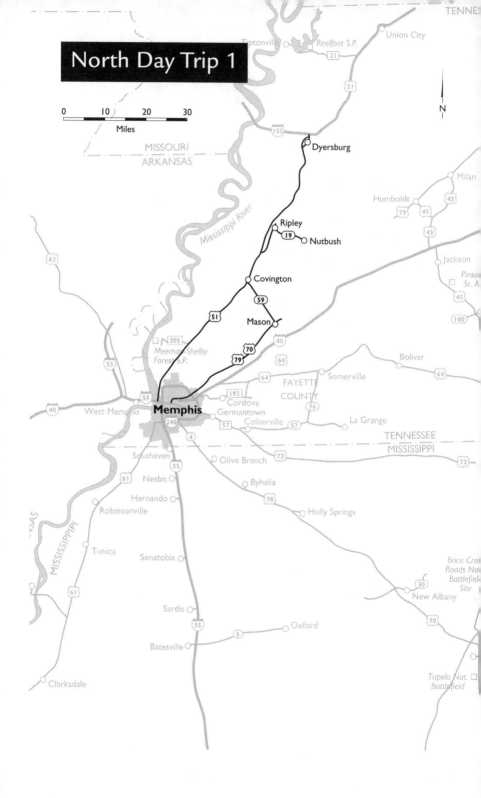

North Day Trip 1

| 0 | 10 | 20 | 30 |
Miles

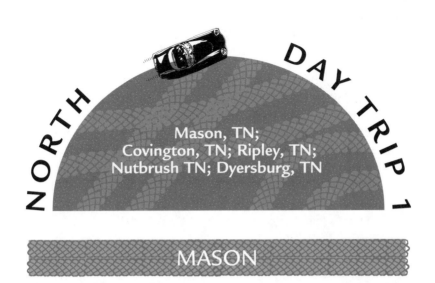
MASON

Following Summer until it becomes US 70/79 north, you'll run into the town of Mason. As you leave Memphis, you'll begin to notice the scenery shift from the hustle and bustle of the city to the serene, picturesque setting of the country. This small town is home to two of the most popular restaurants in all of Tennessee, both featuring the quintessential southern fare of barbecue and fried chicken. Think of Mason as a stop on the way to or from Covington.

WHERE TO EAT

Bozo's. 342 Highway 70, Mason, TN 38018. Barbecue is the main staple on this menu. From chopped pork sandwiches to the ever-popular barbecue salad, Bozo's draws visitors from miles around. The neon sign beckons from the road, and the cozy diner feeling inside allows patrons to enjoy a leisurely meal. If the wait at Bozo's is too long (there aren't too many restaurants in this area), head just down the street to Gus's, one of the most famous chicken joints in America. $$. (901) 294–3400.

    Gus's Fried Chicken. 505 Highway 70, Mason, TN 38018. Gus's has basically one featured menu item, and yes, it's fried chicken. The "restaurant" is nothing more than a shack with linoleum tables and a random mix of plastic chairs, so don't expect much. The waitresses scurry back and forth among the eight or nine tables with paper plates piled high with chicken and Wonder Bread and their hands

wrapped around twenty-ounce Bud longnecks. On weekends the wait is about an hour, so consider getting some chow to go. After your bill is tallied on a legal pad, you'll be asked to pay by cash only. There's no ATM in the area, so plan ahead. Even though the place is a bit of a dive, it's been rated as one of the top meals in the world—worth flying for—by GQ magazine. And because of its "shabby chic" recognition, Gus's has achieved national popularity. Best of all for Memphians, it's only a twenty-minute drive away; you won't even have to take a plane to get there. $$. (901) 294-2028.

COVINGTON

From Mason, take TN 59 northwest to Covington approximately fifty minutes outside Memphis. Once you reach this quiet little town, you'll be charmed by the southern hospitality and easygoing attitude of the locals. Covington is the third largest town in West Tennessee, and was once a part of the Chickasaw Indian Nation. Before they were forced off the land, the Chickasaw lived in several villages made up of log cabins, supporting themselves by farming, fishing, hunting, and trading. In his travels throughout what is now West Tennessee, the Spanish explorer Hernando de Soto came into contact with the Chickasaw Indian Nation—the first white person to do so. Throughout history, the Chickasaw gained a reputation for being ferocious warriors. During the Civil War, many members of the tribe fought for the Confederacy.

WHERE TO GO

Tipton County Chamber of Commerce. 622 South Main Street, Covington, TN 38019. To get maps and information about Covington, stop by the chamber of commerce. (901) 476-9727.

Tipton County Museum—Veterans Memorial and Nature Center. 751 Bert Johnson Avenue, Covington, TN 38019. The museum, which opened in 1998, pays tribute to the veterans of Tipton County while also honoring the spirit of conservation. The largest wildlife park in Tipton County (and one of the county's newest attractions), the nature center celebrates the natural surroundings of West Tennessee. You can tour the twenty-two-acre Covington Wildlife Sanctuary on its breathtaking 0.5-mile nature trail through a natural forest, then view artifacts celebrating the history of West Tennessee's veterans, including uniforms and artillery. While exhibits rotate regularly, the goal of the museum is to bring together history, environmental education, and historic preservation. Open Tuesday through Saturday. Free. (901) 476-0242.

South Main Historic District. 622 South Main Street, Covington, TN 38019. Comprised of more than fifty historic sites, the district is a wonderful fanfare of period buildings. Tours are conducted through the Tipton County Chamber of Commerce, and homes are open for touring each year in September during the Heritage Day Festival. Other stops along the tour include the art-deco Ruffin Theater, the Hotel Lindo, and the Tipton County Courthouse, all of which are on the National Register of Historic Places. Open daily. Free. (901) 476-9727.

WHERE TO SHOP

The Rose Garden. 500 West Burgess, Covington, TN 38019. Located in the barn where owner Ellen Weedman spent her childhood, this shop is quite a treat. It's filled with unusual gifts that reflect either a natural or a Victorian flair; you can also design a custom floral arrangement. After you've shopped in the barn, stroll around the grounds and enjoy the rose and herb garden. If possible, plan a trip to the Rose Garden in October for the shop's Christmas Open House, which draws thousands of visitors each year. But keep in mind that the Rose Garden is closed on Wednesday and Sunday. (901) 476-2662.

Main St. Antiques and Tea Room. 1760 Highway 51, Covington, TN 38019. Off the main thoroughfare in Covington, Main St. Antiques features booths from fifteen dealers in the Tipton County area. Stroll along aisles of gifts, antiques, new and old books, and a terrific collection of furniture. (901) 475-6181.

Old Town Hall. 112 East Court Street, Covington, TN 38019. Browse through a dozen booths featuring a wide array of merchandise. Some of the highlights in Old Town Hall include a selection of reproduction furniture, Brighton accessories, glassware, crystal, silver, hand-painted items, and an extensive collection of antique lamps. (901) 475-0502.

WHERE TO EAT

The Tea Room. 1760 Highway 51, Covington, TN 38019. This snug tearoom is located inside the Main St. Antiques and Tea Room shop (see Where to Shop). Once you've browsed through the antiques and gifts for sale, stop in the tearoom for a delightful lunch. The spot features a weekly variety of plate lunches, but always offers its famous chicken salad and homemade rolls and desserts. While the tearoom is only open Tuesday through Friday and on the first Saturday of each month, you can reserve the room for private parties of groups of twenty or more. Just call in advance to set the menu and make reservations. $-$$; ☐. (901) 475-6181.

Pericos. 105 Mueller Brass Road, Covington, TN 38019. This authentic Mexican restaurant blends the flavors and textures found in traditional Mexican cooking with dishes common in the Southwest. The result is a delightful and colorful variety of carefully prepared meals. Some of the more popular items at Pericos include the grilled shrimp salad, Fiesta Enchiladas, Pericos Fajitas, and chimichanga lunch. In an effort to make this a memorable dining experience in the Midsouth, Pericos bends over backward to provide you with great service. In fact, it says at the bottom of the menu, "If you don't see your favorite combination, let us know and we will be happy to please you." Who could ask for anything more? $-$$; ☐. (901) 475-6300.

WHERE TO STAY

Havenhall Guest House. 183 Houston Gordon Road, Covington, TN 38019. This quaint little bed-and-breakfast has three charming rooms available, and offers a continental breakfast. Enjoy horseback riding, fishing, and the jogging trail, all located on the grounds of the Havenhall Farm. $$-$$$; ☐. (901) 476-7359.

SPECIAL EVENTS

Frazier Park Fun Festival. June. A day of fun for the whole family, the Fun Festival features entertainment, crafts, and games. (901) 476-0242.

Tipton County Fair and Heritage Day Festival. September. Drawing tourists from around the state, the Tipton County Fair features games and rides for kids of all ages. In conjunction with the fair, the residents of Tipton County take part in Heritage Day Festival, paying tribute to the people and places of Tipton County. (901) 476-0242.

    Great Pumpkin Patch Halloween Festival. October. Fun for the whole family, the Great Pumpkin Patch Halloween Festival encourages visitors to take part in pumpkin picking, painting, and game playing. (901) 476-0242.

RIPLEY

From Covington, your next destination is Ripley, Tennessee. Get onto US 51 north and travel a few miles up the road to Ripley, home of some of the most famous tomatoes in Tennessee. In fact, the citizens of Ripley take such pride in their crop that a three-day celebration is dedicated to the tomato: the Lauderdale County Tomato Festival. And you've probably noticed this infamous produce at most every grocery store in town. The area around Ripley was originally inhabited by Chickasaw Indians, who referred to the land as being "nearer heaven" because it's higher in elevation than most of the surrounding area.

WHERE TO GO

Lauderdale County Chamber of Commerce. 103 East Jackson Street, Ripley, TN 38063. Call the chamber of commerce to get additional information about the Lauderdale County Tomato Festival, a three-day festival that features local music and entertainment, food, shooting contests, and the infamous "tomato war." The festival pays tribute to the county's fifty tomato growers, who produce this highly sought-after crop on more than 1,200 acres in Lauderdale County. (901) 635-9541.

    Lauderdale Cellars. 1900 Highway 51 South, Ripley, TN 38063. Winemaker Michael Pace, along with owner Roy Crowder, who is also a local dentist, create some of the most delicious concoctions available in West Tennessee at this local cellar. Together, the pair has created fifteen varieties of wine—from reds, whites, and sweets to the infamous tomato wine, made with 100 percent real tomato juice. Lauderdale Cellars also boasts it's in-house brand, Vintage Vine Marinade, which is available in specialty food stores across the state. Feel free to stroll around the eighteen acres of vineyard, and be sure to browse through the gift and antiques shop before you leave. (731) 635-4321.

Haley House and Museum. 200 Church Street, Henning, TN 38061. It was at the home of his grandparents in Henning that author Alex Haley first heard the tales of his ancestors. He later re-created these poignant stories in his famous book *Roots,* which inspired millions of African Americans to retrace their own family histories. Tour this ten-room home and see how much of the home looked when Haley was a boy. The museum also has an extensive collection of Haley's own personal items. You can purchase Haley's works at the museum and visit his grave—the author is buried in the front yard of the house. (901) 738-2240.

SPECIAL EVENTS

Tomato Festival. July. In honor of the city's most popular produce, citizens take time out of their busy schedules to celebrate the fruits of more than fifty tomato growers' labors. This event features lots of tomato-themed attractions, including the "tomato war." It also gives area entertainers and craftspeople a chance to showcase their talents. (901) 635-9541.

Choctaw Indian Festival. October. Located at the US 51/ TN 87 intersection, the Choctaw Reservation hosts the Choctaw Indian Festival during the last week in October. Native Americans share their culture with visitors by demonstrating Indian skills, traditions, and dances. (901) 738-2951.

NUTBUSH

Nutbush is located just 50 miles northeast of Memphis via US 51. Take the exit for TN 19, veering right off the exit. A number of famous people have their roots in this sleepy southern town. In the early 1800s former slave, community leader, and minister Hardin

Smith was purchased and brought to Haywood County. Smith was a skilled carpenter as well as a minister. He was secretly taught to read and write by his owner's wife, and was also given permission to preach to a slave congregation at Woodlawn Baptist Church in Nutbush. In turn, Smith began teaching members of his slave congregation to read. He also helped with the organization of many of the churches in Nutbush, as well as schools and colleges in the West and Middle Tennessee areas. Smith's legacy has influenced many well-known natives of Nutbush, including the Reverend Clay Evans, Sleepy John Estes, and Tina Turner.

Nutbush/Tina Turner Heritage Center. The Nutbush/Tina Turner Heritage Center welcomes visitors April through October to see the birthplace of the famous singer. The center offers a tour of the heritage trail, fishing, and both indoor and outdoor activities. Because the center is located in a very rural part of West Tennessee, you'll need to call for driving directions and hours of operation. (731) 772-4265.

DYERSBURG

Return to US 51 and continue up north to the quaint town of Dyersburg, Tennessee. This small town is home to a number of unique festivals that make the 70-mile trip from Memphis worth the drive. And each April, as the state tree begins to bloom, citizens of Dyersburg along with visitors from all over the Midsouth join in a celebration known as the Dogwood Festival.

WHERE TO GO

Dyer County Chamber of Commerce. 2000 Commerce Avenue, Dyersburg, TN 38024. To get inside information on the town of Dyersburg, stop by the chamber of commerce. (731) 285-3433.

Dr. Walter E. David Wildlife Museum. 1510 Lake Road, Dyersburg, TN 38024. Housed on the campus of Dyersburg State Community College, this wildlife museum boasts every type of duck found on the Mississippi Flyway. It also has both Kodiak and polar bears. Admission is free. (731) 286-3200.

WHERE TO EAT

Jerry's Little Cedar Store. 2255 St. Johns, Dyersburg, TN 38024. Tucked inside a convenience store, Jerry's offers some of the best sandwiches and hearty lunches around. Choose from fried bologna, Chicago-style hot dogs, or, for the bigger appetite, a slab of ribs. Closed Sunday. $-$$; ☐. (731) 285-9018.

SPECIAL EVENTS

Dogwood Festival and Dogwood Dash. April. Each year Dyersburg comes alive at the Dogwood Festival and Dogwood Dash. The festival has something for everyone, including a golf tournament, beauty pageants, a chili cook-off, an arts and crafts show, and a car show. The Dogwood Dash—featuring a youth run, a health walk, and 5K and 10K races—attracts hundreds of participants from across the country.

The Jimmy Dean Foods Barbecue Festival. May. Part of the Memphis in May barbecue competition, this two-day event includes the cooking of 4,000 pounds of barbecued pork, music, and fun for the family.

Dyer County Fair. September. The fair features a combination of carnival rides, crafts, livestock, horticulture, and antiques exhibits.

McIvers Bluff Founders Day Festival. October. Each year, downtown Dyersburg hosts a celebration of the community's heritage with arts and crafts as well as events and demonstrations that mirror life in Dyer County's early days.

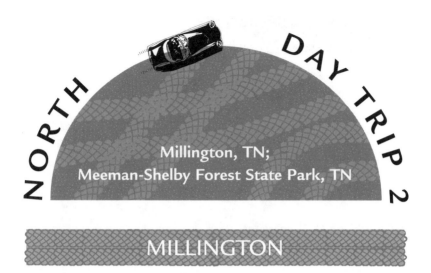

MILLINGTON

US 51 north (actually, northeast) will take you straight through northern Shelby County and into Millington, which hovers just on the south side of the highway about 5 miles north of Memphis. Millington is home of the world's largest inland navy base. It's also, according to the mayor, a city in transition, with widely expanding subdivisions and quickly growing commerce.

WHERE TO GO

Millington Chamber of Commerce. 7743 Church Street, Millington, TN 38053. The city chamber of commerce is open Monday through Friday to assist you with information about the Millington area. (901) 872–1486.

Millington USA Stadium. 4351 Babe Howard Boulevard, Millington, TN 38053. International recognition makes USA Stadium Millington's pride and joy. In less than a decade, this stadium has hosted 166 baseball games with teams from eighteen different countries. USA Stadium has also hosted fourteen national championships, including decisive victory games in American Legion, AAU, NABF, and Junior College World Series play. If you're remotely interested in baseball, stop by the stadium to take a look around. There's a gift shop with a huge selection of T-shirts and memorabilia. If you plan to go in spring or summer, check the Web site, which maintains a schedule of events and tournaments: www.usabaseballstadium.org. (901) 872–8326.

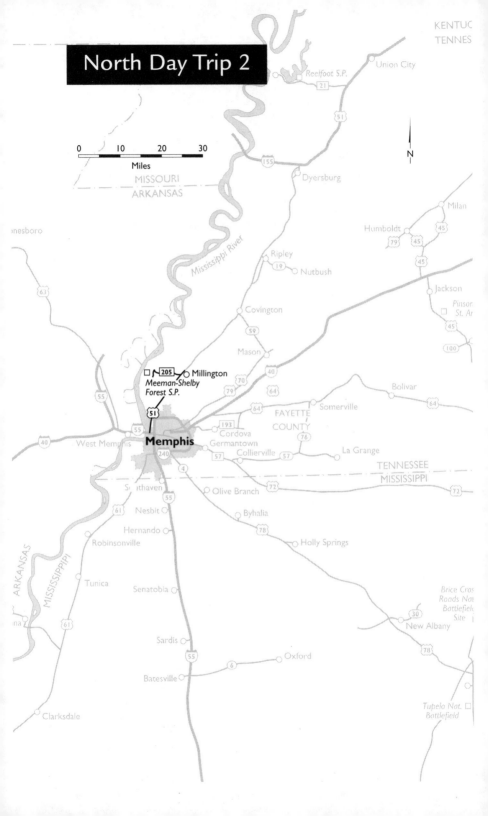

North Day Trip 2

0 10 20 30
Miles

KENTUC
TENNES

Reelfoot S.P.   Union City
21
51
155
MISSOURI   Dyersburg
ARKANSAS

Milan

Humboldt   45
79   45
45
Jackson
Pinson
St. Ar
45
100

Ripley
esboro   19   Nutbush

63   Covington

59   Mason   40
Bolivar
64
70
79
64   64
205   Millington   Somerville
Meeman-Shelby   193   FAYETTE
Forest S.P.   Cordova   COUNTY
51   76
55   Germantown   La Grange
Memphis   57   Collierville   57
West Memphis   240
40   4   TENNESSEE
MISSISSIPPI
72   72
uthaven   Olive Branch
55
61   Nesbit   Byhalia
Hernando   78
Robinsonville   Holly Springs

ARKANSAS
MISSISSIPPI
Tunica   *Brice Cros*
Roads Nat
Senatobia   *Battlefiel*
Site
30
New Albany
Sardis   78
55
6   Oxford
Batesville

Clarksdale   *Tupelo Nat.*
Battlefield

Memphis International MotorSports Park. 5500 Taylor Forge Drive, Millington, TN 38053. The park is located on Fite Road between US 51 and Raleigh-Millington Road: you can't miss it. This 600-acre, four-track park hosts professional and amateur auto racing weekly during spring and summer. It's serious business at Memphis MotorSports Park, where racers compete on a 1.8-mile road course, a drag strip, and a dirt oval. Call ahead for the schedule. (901) 358-7223.

Strand Music Hall. 7979 Wilkinsville, Millington, TN 38053. The Strand Theatre was built in 1939 to show movies, but for the last twenty years or so, it's been a music hall featuring gospel music on Friday night and a live band with country dancing Saturday night. Although regulars make up most of the weekend crowd, guests from miles come to listen to the beat of Billy Owen's All-American Band and two-step or line-dance with the Country Music Showcase. The Strand advertises itself as "good family entertainment" with a "hometown atmosphere." You won't find any alcohol there, and children of all ages are welcome (nine and under free; everyone else pays $4.00 entry). (901) 872-1420.

WHERE TO EAT

Karen's Deli-N-Diner. 5433 Navy Road, Millington, TN 38053. You'll get real home cookin' at Karen's for breakfast and lunch. The menu offers the standard deli and diner fare of sandwiches, salads, and soups, along with a different lunch special each day. With the special you get not two but three vegetables and a meat. Nearly all the meals are under $5.00; most are about $3.00. Karen's closes at 2:00 P.M. after the lunch crowd, so make sure you get there in time. $; □. (901) 872-3354.

SPECIAL EVENTS

MidSouth Airshow. May. Every other spring for the past several years, Millington has hosted the MidSouth Airshow, sponsored by the MidSouth Foundation, Inc. It features a variety of demonstrations, including aerobatic maneuvers, Big Foot (truck) performances, and military and civilian fly-bys. (901) 753-1653.

Flag Day Celebration. July 3. Flag Day in Millington falls on the eve of the Fourth of July. It's full of patriotism and education about the American flag. Special attractions in years past have included demonstrations by the Memphis Parachute Club, the Navy Flying Rifles Drill Team, and the Marine Corps Color Guard. The city of Millington sponsors the event. (901) 872–6252.

International Goat Days Family Festival. September. What started out as a goat chariot race has turned into a full-fledged family festival with music and food competitions, a petting zoo and rodeo, and all kinds of antiques and crafts for sale. It's usually held the second weekend in September, but call ahead or check the Web site for exact dates: www.internationalgoatdays.com. (901) 872–4559.

MEEMAN-SHELBY FOREST STATE PARK

Shelby State Park borders the east bank of the Mississippi River. If you're coming from Memphis, take I-40 north to exit 2-A, then turn right. After six stoplights, make a left onto Watkins Road and another left when it dead-ends. Drive 1 mile to a four-way stop, where you'll see Shelby Forest General Store (your last stop for picnic supplies). Turn right at the store, go 1 mile, and turn left into the park. If you're coming from US 51 in Millington, take TN 205 west. It's about a five- or ten-minute drive, and you'll see signs guiding you into the park. More than 60 percent of the 13,000-acre park is hardwood forest, including oak, cypress, and tupelo trees. Spend the day enjoying the natural environment, which also includes two lakes and hiking trails, or bring your boat to the ramp and float along the river while you watch the deer, turkeys, beavers, and birds.

WHERE TO GO

Meeman-Shelby Forest State Park. 910 Riddick Road, Millington, TN 38053. The most popular thing to do at the park is hike. With more than 20 miles of hiking trails, you can hike all day and still have some untraversed trails for next time. You can also bring your dog—as long as it's on a leash. The hiking trails are open year-round and are wheelchair accessible. The park also maintains basic biking trails, though not mountain bike trails. Between Memorial and Labor Day each summer, visitors can swim in the park's pool, which after a year of renovations reopened in the summer of 2001 boasting major improvements in safety and fun. If you call ahead, Park Ranger Bubba McCain can give you the lowdown on what's happening in his neck of the woods. www.state.tn.us/environment/parks/meeman/index.html. (901) 876-5215.

Meeman Museum and Nature Center. The nature center is the park's hub and is open year-round on weekends. From mid-April to mid-November, it's open every day of the week from 11:00 A.M. to 7:00 p.m. The center sponsors exhibits, including live snakes, stuffed animals, a "touch table," and Native American history. It also offers a variety of special programs and activities, such as making bird-feeders and homemade ice cream, pontoon boat rides, and nature videos. (901) 876-5215.

Poplar Tree Lake fishing. Poplar Tree Lake is 125 acres of large-mouth bass, bream, and catfish just waiting for your bait. There's a boat dock, and johnboats are available for rental; most visitors simply fish from the pier or bank, though. Keep in mind that in order to fish, you must have a park fishing permit (available at the park office) and a valid Tennessee fishing license if you're sixteen years of age or older. (901) 876-5215.

WHERE TO EAT

Picnic pavilions. With the assistance of a park map, obtainable at the museum and nature center, you can find 300 picnic tables with area grills all throughout the park. Near each pavilion are rest rooms, water fountains, and a playground. If you have a large group, you can call ahead—up to one year—for reservations. (901) 876-5215.

WHERE TO STAY

Cabins at Poplar Tree Lake. At the shore of the lake, surrounded by woods, are six two-bedroom cabins, which can accommodate six people per cabin. Each offers a kitchen and television, linens, and a fireplace with wood. Call up to a year in advance to make reservations. Wheelchair-accessible cabins are available. $$. (901) 876-5215.

Camping. If you're a real nature lover, you may want to forgo the modern conveniences of cabin living and camp out in the "wild." Scattered throughout the park are forty-nine campsites, all with grills, water fountains, and electrical and water hookups. You can still get a hot shower in the bathhouses. Once again, you can make reservations up to a year ahead of time (recommended during holidays). (901) 876–5215.

SPECIAL EVENTS

Junior Fishing Rodeo. May. This Poplar Tree Lake fishing competition runs from 8:00 a.m. until noon and awards young anglers a variety of prizes, including trophies. (901) 876–5201.

Summerfest. June. This is the park's all-around nature appreciation day. Nature enthusiasts from the Midsouth join for hikes, along with educational programs and workshops, offered by expert conservationists. (901) 876–5201.

Chickasaw Bluffs Appreciation Day. September. Chickasaw Bluffs Day is another chance to appreciate the beauty and history of the bluffs' natural environment, including its wildlife. Follow park experts as they show and teach you about edible and homeopathic plants of the bluffs. (901) 876–5201.

James Logan Colbert Living Day. October. Billed by the park as "Frontier Tennessee Revisited," James Logan Colbert Living Day is full of rustic renditions of what life was like in the eighteenth and nineteenth centuries. Hosts even rally the crowd into playing the hundred-year-old games of our Tennessee heritage. (901) 876–5201.

UNION CITY

Union City is a perfect escape to the great outdoors. At the foot of Reelfoot Lake, there are plenty of activities for the entire family. Travel up US 51 north until you reach TN 78. Then take the I-155 east ramp toward Union City. I-155 east becomes US 51 north. Turn left onto TN 21. You'll find yourself in the controversial town of Union City, home of the stolen courthouse. Generations have passed down the story of how the citizens of Union City captured the county seat from the town of Troy—which was designated the Obion County seat in 1823—with the help of Civil War hero Davy Crockett.

WHERE TO GO

Obion County Chamber of Commerce. 214 East Church Street, Union City, TN 38261. Stop in the chamber of commerce for brochures and information on local attractions in Obion County. (901) 885-0211.

Dixie Gun Works. 1412 West Reelfoot Avenue, Union City, TN 38261. This thriving business had its humble beginning in an old coal shed back in the mid-1950s. Today it boasts an incredible selection of antique firearms, many of which were made circa 1900. In addition, Dixie Gun Works has an extensive line of replica guns and reenactment costumes. In fact, when the movies *Glory* and *Last of the Mohicans* were being filmed, producers enlisted the help of Dixie Gun Works to arm the actors with the guns men would have used during the respective time periods.

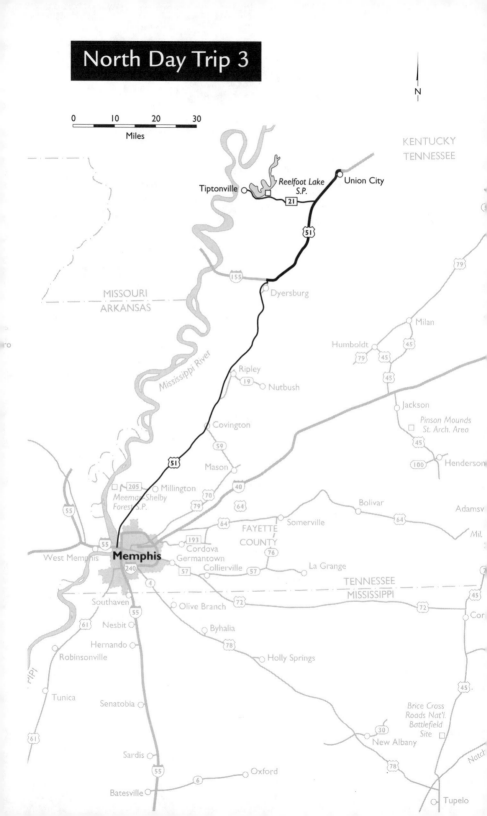

North Day Trip 3

N

| 0 | 10 | 20 | 30 |
Miles

KENTUCKY
TENNESSEE

Reelfoot Lake
S.P.

Tiptonville   Union City

21

51

MISSOURI
ARKANSAS

155

Dyersburg

Milan

79

Humboldt

79   45

Mississippi River

Ripley

45

19   Nutbush

Jackson

Pinson Mounds
St. Arch. Area

Covington

45

59

Mason

100   Henderson

51

40

205   Millington

Meeman-Shelby
Forest S.P.

70   79

64

Bolivar

55

64

Adamsv

Mil.

FAYETTE
COUNTY   Somerville

64

West Memphis

Memphis

193

Cordova

Germantown

57   Collierville   57

76

La Grange

TENNESSEE
MISSISSIPPI

240

4

55

Southaven

72

45

61   Nesbit

Olive Branch

Byhalia

72

Cor

Hernando

78

Robinsonville

Holly Springs

45

Tunica

Senatobia

Brice Cross
Roads Nat'l.
Battlefield
Site

61

30

New Albany

Sardis

55

Oxford

6

78

Tupelo

Batesville

Natc

Dixie Gun Works has expanded into showcasing antique vehicles as well. On the grounds is the Old Car Museum, with restored vehicles including an early-1900s Maxwell two-passenger. The museum also features thousands of antique automobile accessories, as well as outboard engines and an extensive collection of train whistles. (901) 885-0561.

Obion County Museum. 1004 Edwards Street, Union City, TN 38261. The museum opened in 1970, when it first showcased the McNatt Collection of antique toys and tools at the county fair. Since then it has grown to include a log cabin and a one-room schoolhouse, along with myriad historic photos and a special section devoted to Native American artifacts.

While the museum hosts a number of exhibits throughout the year, its permanent collection includes a 1917 buggy donated by T. C. Sowell, who traded his sheep for the buggy, and a miniature Obion County Railroad network that features a replica of the Union City–Rives–Gibbs triangle of the 1950s. Next to the museum is a classic two-room log cabin that has been restored by the Reelfoot Builders Association. Hours of operation are Saturday and Sunday afternoon. (901) 885-6774.

WHERE TO EAT

Dixie Barn. 1315 Old Troy Highway, Union City, TN 38261. This dining establishment was built in the late 1980s and has become a mainstay for locals in Union City. Reminiscent of a barn, the kitchen renders all kinds of tasty treats. Some menu favorites are the baby back ribs, the ten-ounce rib eye, and the chicken strips dinner. Still, one of the unique and most popular items remains the country ham melt sandwich. $–$$; □. (901) 885-3663.

Flippen's Fruit Farm and Hillbilly Barn. 3734 West Shawtown Road, Troy, TN 38260. Hidden a few miles outside Union City, Flippen's has become world famous. The farm was originally used to grow cotton, but in the 1950s the Flippens began growing fruit. The rest, as they say, is history. The farm focuses on two fruits: apples and peaches. There are eight varieties of apples and twenty-eight of peaches. The Hillbilly Barn sells homemade fried pies and peach ice cream, dried fruits, candies (regular and sugar-free), nuts, honeys, and syrups. In addition to the pies, Flippen's also serves groups a tasty all-you-can-eat buffet featuring fish, ham, onion rings, slaw, white beans, apples, and hush puppies. (901) 538-2933.

WHERE TO STAY

Hospitality House. 1221 West Reelfoot Avenue, Union City, TN 38261. With seventy-two rooms, a meeting room, and a pool, the Hospitality House is a convenient stop for groups or families. Each room comes with a microwave and refrigerator; a continental breakfast is served daily in the motel's lobby. $-$$; □. (731) 885-6610.

TIPTONVILLE

From Union City, get back onto TN 21 and travel a few miles south to Tiptonville, Tennessee, located on the western shore of Reelfoot Lake. The lake is believed to be a product of a powerful earthquake that shook the foundation around the early 1800s. Whether you enjoy fishing, hunting, or bird-watching, this respite is the place to be. Of course, if you enjoy great food in a peaceful setting, you won't be disappointed, either. Tiptonville is home to a number of fun, family-oriented lodging destinations, as well as a place where outdoorspeople seem to flock.

WHERE TO GO

Reelfoot Lake State Park. Route 1, Box 2345, Tiptonville, TN 38079. Legend has it that Reelfoot Lake was a production of the infamous New Madrid earthquake in 1811. Reportedly, a crevice opened between the Mississippi River and Reelfoot Lake's cypress bottoms; locals say the river flowed backward for three days, causing the lake to form.

The park is one of the greatest hunting and fishing preserves in the nation. The park itself encompasses 25,000 acres (15,000 of which are underwater) and is the only natural lake within the state of Tennessee. It lodges almost every species of shore- and wading bird, as well as deer and turkeys. The lake is also a natural fish hatchery, which draws eagles to its grounds for feeding. You can find a wide variety of flowering and nonflowering plants within the park, but cypress trees dominate the lake's shore.

In addition to eagle-watching, which is at its peak in February, the park offers a variety of outdoor activities. Fishing and hunting top the list, and it's important to note that Reelfoot Lake is the last lake in Tennessee with no creel limit. It's also a popular spot for hunting ducks, deer, squirrels, rabbits, and raccoons. Visitors are also encouraged to hike or canoe this natural oasis. (731) 253-7756.

WHERE TO SHOP

Eagle Tree Gallery. Route 1, Box 520, Tiptonville, TN 38079. The gallery houses a unique collection of Native American art and handicraft items, which are produced by more than thirty Native American tribes. Some of the unique items you'll find at Eagle Tree Gallery include dream catchers, mandalas, medicine wheels, and headdresses, along with dolls from the Navajo, Huron, Apache, and Hopi tribes and fetishes from the Zuni. Browse the incredible selection of jewelry, both silver and gold, inlay and needlepoint styles. The gallery also has a wide array of interior decorating items such as hand-painted feather and skin wall hangings, baskets, pottery, cradle boards, and Navajo rugs. (731) 253-8652.

WHERE TO EAT

Boyette's. Route 1, Box 71, Tiptonville, TN 38079. Located on the shore of Reelfoot Lake, Boyette's had its humble beginnings as a country grocery store and sandwich shop. Today it has grown to seat 300 guests with three private dining rooms—and it's no wonder. The simple yet satisfying menu keeps visitors coming back for more. Some of the more popular items on the menu include the homemade onion rings; chicken, turkey, or pork potatoes; burgers; and ribs. And to top it all off, there's home-style peach cobbler for dessert. $-$$; □. (731) 253-7516.

Blue Bank Fish House and Grill. Lake Drive, Tiptonville, TN 38079. This popular spot is frequented by fishermen and -women from all around the world. A favorite spot of well-known angler Bill Dance, the Blue Bank Fish House and Grill has all the makings of a great meal. In fact, he wrote about the spot that it "always leaves you wishing you had room for just one more bite." For breakfast, try the baked apple pancakes or sausage and sawmill gravy atop hot buttered biscuits. For dinner, enjoy locally caught fried quail, frog legs, or grilled steaks or chops, and choose from side items like baked apples, soup beans, or a salad topped with Blue Bank blue cheese. $–$$; ☐. (731) 253-6878.

WHERE TO STAY

Blue Basin Cove B&B. Route 1, Box 2300, Tiptonville, TN 38079. Whether you've planned an action-packed weekend of eagle-watching, or are looking for a serene getaway, the Blue Basin Cove B&B will meet your lodging needs with a variety of rooms, including suites. Once you're ready to rise and shine, proprietor Nancy Moore will help you plan your day. She can arrange for a guided tour of the lake itself, or an outing of hunting, fishing, or bird-watching. Advance notice is recommended for guided tours.

If you're visiting the lake for fishing, Blue Basin Cove offers the use of a covered boatslip and fish-cleaning area. Electrical outlets are handy for battery recharging, and there's a freezer for your catch. If bird-watching is your thing, you've picked a perfect spot, because the Blue Basin is located on the Mississippi Flyway and is just 1 mile from the Black Bayou Waterfowl Refuge. Or you can take a tour of the heron/egret rookery—just let Nancy know in advance. $$–$$$; ☐. (731) 253-9064.

Blue Bank Resort. Lake Drive, Tiptonville, TN 38079. Blue Bank offers three different types of lodging sure to meet every need and host every size group. The first is the Hunters Lodge, located at the Blue Bank Resort Marina, which has a homey feel with an astounding view of the lake. It can house up to nineteen people comfortably and has its own kitchen, dining area, picnic area, and private fishing access, making it perfect for a family vacation or a getaway for a group of anglers.

Another choice is the Marina Lodging, located on the edge of the water. In addition to comfortable rooms, the Marina has a surrounding boardwalk deck where you can swim, fish, or sit and watch the world go by. Inside is an enormous game room where guests can play pool, chess, checkers, or cards. When you get thirsty, you won't have to travel far—right inside the game room is a cozy little bar.

Finally, you can enjoy Blue Bank's resort rooms, located right in the middle of all the action. Whether you're in town to watch the eagles or go fishing, boating, or hiking, you'll be close to it all. The resort rooms are also conveniently located near the Fish House and Grill. $$-$$$; ☐. (731) 253-6878.

Reelfoot Lake State Park. Route 1, Box 2345, Tiptonville, TN 38079. If you prefer to stay on the campgrounds, Reelfoot Lake State Park has a wide variety of accommodations available, from the modern convenience of the Airpark Inn to the scenic panorama of the rustic campsites. $-$$; ☐. (731) 253-7756; for reservations, (800) 250-8617.

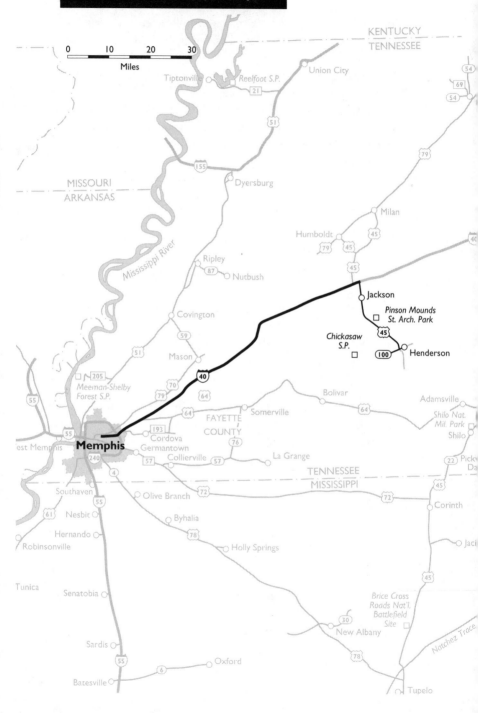

Northeast Day Trip 1

N

Miles
0   10   20   30

KENTUCKY
TENNESSEE

MISSOURI
ARKANSAS

Tiptonville

Reelfoot S.P.

Union City

Dyersburg

Mississippi River

Milan

Humboldt

Ripley

Nutbush

Covington

Jackson

Pinson Mounds
St. Arch. Park

Chickasaw
S.P.

Henderson

Mason

Meeman-Shelby
Forest S.P.

Bolivar

Adamsville

Shilo Nat.
Mil. Park

Shilo

est Memphis

Memphis

Cordova
Germantown
Collierville

FAYETTE
COUNTY

Somerville

La Grange

Pick
Da

TENNESSEE
MISSISSIPPI

Southaven

Olive Branch

Corinth

Nesbit

Byhalia

Hernando

Robinsonville

Holly Springs

Jac

Tunica

Senatobia

Brice Cross
Roads Nat'l.
Battlefield
Site

Sardis

New Albany

Natchez Trace

Batesville

Oxford

Tupelo

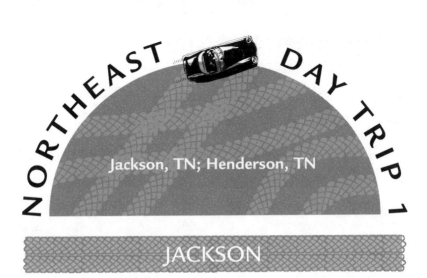

JACKSON

Jackson, Tennessee, lies just about an hour outside Memphis; it's a straight shot up I-40 east. Aside from being the home of legendary rock-and-roller Carl Perkins and train engineer Casey Jones, Jackson maintains the perfect balance between big-city attractions and small-town charm. It dates back to the 1800s, when settlers selected a former Chickasaw Indian hunting ground along the Forked Deer River to form a community. At the time they named their settlement Alexandria, but the name was later changed to Jackson in honor of President Andrew Jackson. Since its beginning, Jackson has enjoyed enormous growth and prosperity, and was ranked by *Restaurant Business* magazine as second among United States cities in restaurant growth in 1998. *Forbes* magazine referred to Jackson as "a top 25 city for the future," and with all of the hustle and bustle in town, it's no wonder.

WHERE TO GO

Jackson Area Chamber of Commerce. 197 Auditorium Street, Jackson, TN 38301. Before hitting all the hot spots in Jackson, stop by the chamber of commerce and get area maps and brochures. (731) 423-2200.

West Tennessee Farmer's Market. Lafayette and Shannon Street junction, Jackson, TN. The farmer's market is a popular spot for growers and buyers from all over West Tennessee. Produce is grown locally and sold each week based on availability. Crops are brought in seasonally; you'll also find a variety of canned goods, preserves, and other homemade items. Open daily Monday through Saturday.

Jackson Greyhound Station. 407 East Main Street, Jackson, TN 38301. The site where several motion pictures were filmed, the Jackson Greyhound Station is one of the nation's few remaining 1950s-era bus stations. Filled with nostalgia, this station remains fully functional. Visitors to the station are greeted with distinctive porcelain tiles on the outside of the building and enter through the original wooden doors. Inside, the station is filled with large curved windows, and ornate medallions cover the ceiling vents. (731) 427–1573.

Casey Jones Home and Railroad Museum. 40 Casey Jones Lane, Jackson, TN 38305. Railroad man Casey Jones gained notoriety when, on April 30, 1900, he died heroically in a train wreck. It's said that his attempt to slow the train saved the lives of all the passengers; tragically, Jones was the only person to die. Tour the home and museum, and see railroad artifacts from the turn of the twentieth century, when riding the rails was the most popular means of transportation. Discover how railroading has evolved through the generations in two 25-foot model-train displays in a restored 1890s mail car. And visit the home of Casey Jones, which has been restored to its appearance at the time of Jones's death. Open daily; there's a charge for admission. (800) 748–9588.

Electro Chalybeate Well. 604 South Royal Street, Jackson, TN 38301. Located in the middle of town, this well was discovered in the late 1800s, when workers ran across a phenomenal underground river of mineral water while constructing Jackson's first modern waterworks. Once noted for curing "internal ailments," the well remains a popular attraction. The well is under an 1800s-style gazebo and is surrounded by a small park. (731) 422–7209.

Pringles Park. 3241 Ridgecrest Road, Jackson, TN 38305. Come visit the Diamond Jaxx in their home stadium, Pringles Park, and take in some AA baseball family fun. Pringles Park is one of the newest stadiums in the country, boasting 6,200 seats. The park was named in honor of the nation's only Pringles plant, which is located in Jackson. The Diamond Jaxx play a seventy-home-game season, and each game promises to be special with events such as fireworks, contests, and promotions to keep fans in these stands. The season runs April through September. (731) 664–2020.

World's Largest Collection of Rare Porcelain Teapots. 309 South College Street, Trenton, TN 38382. Housed in Trenton City Hall, this collection features more than 500 rare "night light" porcelain teapots. This remarkable assortment has been collected from all over the world. If you're in the area and the hall is closed, run across the street to the fire department—they can provide access during nonbusiness hours. Open daily. Free. (731) 855–2013.

Pinson Mounds State Archeological Park. 460 Ozier Road, Pinson, TN 38310. Just ten minutes outside Jackson, this sequence of mounds is nearly 2,000 years old. Self-guided tours are available along the trails, and the park has a museum and visitor center that has been constructed to look like a mound. The mounds were home to tribes of Mississippian Indians, and the museum provides replicas of how their villages once looked. Open daily. Admission charge. (731) 988–5614.

WHERE TO SHOP

Sisters Boutique. 31 A Wiley Parker Road, Jackson, TN 38305. If you love buying clothes that are unique and fun, this is the place for you. Sisters carries a wide range of outfits, but rarely more than a few sizes of each article, which means you won't run into yourself once you piece together an outfit. Sisters also carries an extensive range of jewelry and accessories. Open daily. (731) 668–7948.

Edenton Etc. 24 Federal Drive, Jackson, TN 38305. Shopping at Edenton is an experience like no other: All the latest trends from the New York runways have somehow been tucked inside this eclectic store. Clothes, jewelry, shoes, and accessories reveal a fun, funky array of styles. And don't miss all of the incredible home accessories in the back of the store—many are the creations of the owner's daughter. Open daily. (731) 660–6070.

Casey Jones Village. 40 Casey Jones Lane, Jackson, TN 38305. The village is home to myriad shops, including the Wildlife in Wood Studio, where master carver Dee Moss renders a number of wooden masterpieces. You'll also find Southern Magnolia gift shop, Fantasy Cutlery East, and the Alpine Christmas and Gift Shop; stop by the Southwest Tennessee Tourist Information Center and the Casey

Jones Southern Junction to get your fill of Tennessee souvenirs, too. As part of the Casey Jones Village, you'll want to visit the Old Country Store, where you'll find a variety of candies, collectibles, and gifts from yesteryear. (800) 748-9588.

WHERE TO EAT

Dumplin's of Jackson. 31 C Wiley Parker Road, Jackson, TN 38305. After you've shopped at Sisters, stop next door at Dumplin's. It alone is worth the drive to Jackson! The menu features such items as chicken and dumplins, pork tenderloin, and lemon pepper chicken; a different casserole is prepared each day. Best of all, you get to savor the sinfully wonderful homemade rolls and honey butter that are served with every entree. A separate dinner menu offers larger portions of the lunch entrees, in addition to items like shrimp scampi, Smothered Malibu Chicken, and a filet. And save room for dessert: Dumplin's tempts you with selections like homemade apple dumpling, caramel upside-down cake, Chocolate Majesty, and the Snickers Blitz Cheesecake. $$; ☐. (731) 664-4959.

Old Country Store. 56 Casey Jones Lane, Jackson, TN 38305. Offering country cooking at its finest, the Old Country Store has both entree items and buffets. Serving breakfast, lunch, and dinner, the store at Casey Jones Village renders ample portions of the traditional meat and three. Of course, if you opt for the buffet, you'll enjoy a delicious variety of down-home delectables night and day. The breakfast buffet features grits, eggs, apples, ham, bacon, and sausage; at dinner you can select from roasts, fried chicken, a number of vegetables, breads, salads, and dessert. $-$$; ☐. (731) 668-6889.

Bubba's Bagels and the Market. 2273 North Highland Avenue, Jackson, TN 38305. Perfect for breakfast or any other meal, Bubba's offers a tasty assortment of bagels, muffins, and more. For lunch, try an Upstream (lox, onion, tomato, and cream cheese on a bagel) or the Sorry Charlie, a house-made tuna salad bagel. If you bring the kids, they'll probably want the Elvis Goldstein, a bagel topped with peanut butter and banana slices. And to top it all off, Bubba's offers almost a dozen specialty drinks, including coffee drinks. $-$$; ☐. (731) 661-0088.

Suede's. 2263 North Highland Avenue, Jackson, TN 38305. Suede's restaurant is the spot in Jackson for local flair. The Jackson hangout is named for the famous song "Blue Suede Shoes," written by native Jacksonian Carl Perkins. The restaurant is filled with memorabilia paying tribute to the late Perkins—and once you're through looking, you can order from a wide array of southern treats. The catfish and barbecue are constant favorites, served with sides of hush puppies, beans, and slaw; or you can try the burger and fries. $$; ☐. (731) 664-1956.

Brooksie's Barn. 561 Oil Well Road, Jackson, TN 38301. Brooksie's Barn is tucked away from the hustle of the city and known not just for its serene setting, but also for its great service and food. When you enter Brooksie's, you're sure to feel right at home. And many tables have a pleasant view of the pond and woods, making the restaurant tops in atmosphere, too. Then there's the food: Brooksie's specializes in country cooking, but the most raved-about item on the menu is the chicken and dumplings. Locals say, hands down, this dish just can't be beat. So stop in and see for yourself what makes Brooksie's a favorite escape from the busy streets of Jackson. $$; ☐. (731) 664-2276.

Baker's Rack. 100 East Baltimore, Jackson, TN 38301. Owner Elaine West had a vision for the Baker's Rack long before it ever actually came into existence. Her husband owned a convenience store, and for years she made baked goods to sell out of his store. When a space became available downtown, she jumped at the chance to make the dream of owning her own place a reality. Starting with a menu of baked goods, Elaine now serves a wide variety of plate lunches, quiches, and, of course, her scrumptious home-baked goodies. $-$$; ☐. (731) 424-6163.

WHERE TO STAY

Four Points Hotel by Sheraton. 2267 North Highland Avenue, Jackson, TN 38305. Enjoy a taste of England right in the center of West Tennessee. Recognized for its unusual design, this Sheraton-owned hotel is furnished throughout with authentic English antiques, beveled-glass doors, and British-inspired landscaping. Four Points Hotel has a number of room plans to choose from and 103 available rooms, including the Parlor King and Executive Suites.

There's a pool on the premises and a full health spa next door. Each room comes with TV, dataport, coffeemaker, and iron. Some suites have fireplaces, patios, refrigerators, and microwaves. (731) 668–1571.

Highland Place B&B. 519 North Highland, Jackson, TN 38301. Owners and innkeepers Cindy and Bill Pflaum invite you to visit their B&B, claiming that "from the time you enter the main foyer, until you leave for home, you will be pampered in just the right ways." Known for its beauty and structure, Highland Place was chosen as the Designer Showhouse for West Tennessee in 1995. During that time, twenty-five interior designers and three landscape artists spent months giving this mansion, which was originally built in 1911, a complete makeover. On April 1, 1995, Highland Place was ready for the public with a bright, fresh look that showed off the total face-lift of one of Jackson's finest mansions. There's a living room, library, and foyer to welcome guests. And of course the dining room is one of the more popular features of Highland Place: Not only do Cindy and Bill serve guests a gracious southern breakfast, but they will also provide a meal for up to twenty-four people if given enough advance notice. This makes Highland Place a great place for family gatherings, business events, or other special occasions. Once you've had your fill of food, mosey into one of the four tastefully decorated rooms and suites. Each has its own private bath. $$$; ☐. (731) 427–1472.

SPECIAL EVENTS

Women's NAIA Basketball Championships. March. The championships are one of the city's top tourist events, drawing more than 40,000 people to the weeklong event. (731) 425–8390.

Taste of Jackson. March. Jackson is noted for its growing restaurant population, and this is an excellent way to get a sample of cooking from a plethora of local eateries. Housed in the Jackson Civic Center, the fund raiser offers aisles and aisles of tempting treats. All money raised is designated for March of Dimes research. (731) 668–1023.

Shannon Street Blues and Heritage Festival. May–June. This fund-raiser for the Jackson Downtown Development Corporation takes place annually at the West Tennessee Farmer's Market. Visitors enjoy listening to top blues acts right in the heart of historic down-town Jackson. The festival also includes a long list of other events, including a barbecue contest and fishing festival. (731) 427-7573.

Forked Deer Festival. May. This festival gets its name from the Forked Deer River and its tributaries, which run through West Tennessee. The festival is centered on the heritage of West Tennessee, giving nod to the fact that Jackson was called Port Jackson in the 1800s because of its location along the river. The event includes a carnival along with national entertainment, folk artists, and a children's area. (731) 427-1565.

West Tennessee State Fair. July–August. Held in Jackson Fairgrounds Park, the fair includes a number of games, exhibits, and pageants. (731) 425-8384.

Archeofest. September. This free event takes place at Pinson Mounds State Park, an ancient Native American dwelling place, and celebrates Native American heritage. Events include arts and crafts such as loom weaving, pottery, basketry, quillwork, and flute making. Archeofest also provides a forum for storytelling, dance performances, tool and weapon demonstrations, nature programs, and hay-wagon tours. (731) 988-5614.

Great Casey Jones Balloon Classic. September–October. This hot-air ballooning event is put on yearly by the Jackson Kiwanis Club on the grounds of the McKellar-Sipes Regional Airport. (731) 427-4431.

Britton Lane Battle Reenactment. September. This reenactment takes place every other year, and is designed to remind onlookers of the Civil War battle that was waged here in 1862. In addition to the reenactment, there's a period church service, a dance, and other festivities. (731) 668-7794.

African Street Festival. September. Every Labor Day weekend festivalgoers celebrate the African heritage of West Tennesseans. A scattering of vendors offer arts, crafts, clothing, and food. Live entertainment is provided in styles ranging from African dance to modern gospel and rap. (731) 422-3973.

Lambuth Area Neighborhood Association Holiday Fundraiser. December. Residents around Lambuth College hold this annual event to help preserve the architectural and historic authenticity of the area. The Holiday Fundraiser includes a home tour, a holiday tea, homemade lunches, and live entertainment. (731) 427-6608.

HENDERSON

After leaving Jackson, return to US 45 and travel south about 17 miles; turn left onto TN 100 to enter Henderson, Tennessee, home of Chickasaw State Park. This campground is located on top of some of the highest terrain in West Tennessee.

WHERE TO GO

Chamber of Commerce. 130 Main Street, Henderson, TN 37213. Stop in Henderson's chamber of commerce before heading to the park to ask questions or get information on the trails of Chickasaw State Park. (731) 989-5222.

Chickasaw State Park. 20 Cabin Lane, Henderson, TN 38340. Chickasaw State Park covers 1,280 acres and adjoins state forest land. Within the park itself are close to 100 miles of trails that lead into the neighboring forest for either hiking or mountain biking. Chickasaw also offers horse trails and a horse campground, called the Wrangler campsite. And it's a favorite spot for fishing. Some of the more popular catches include bass, catfish, crappies, and bluegills. Paddleboats can be rented; private boats and motorized boats are not allowed. In addition to these outdoor activities, facilities for a number of competitive sports are available, including swimming, tennis, archery, and all kinds of ball games. A new Jack Nicklaus-designed golf course is also available. Because you're sure to work up an appetite participating in all these activities, the park includes an enchanting spot for picnicking. (731) 989-5141.

WHERE TO STAY

Chickasaw State Park. 20 Cabin Lane, Henderson, TN 38340. Overnight accommodations include thirteen cottages on the park grounds, an RV campground, a tent campground, and the horse campground. Each area comes with tables, grills, modern bathhouses/rest rooms, and playgrounds. But please keep in mind that camping is allowed only in designated areas. $-$$; □. (731) 989-5141.

PARIS

For a small town, there's a lot going on in Paris, Tennessee. Home to the Clarksville Speedway and myriad parks and resorts, as well being just miles away from the National Boy Scout Museum, this town seems to have been built for the young at heart. To reach Paris, follow I-40 to Jackson, Tennessee, and take US 45 bypass north. Remain on US 45, then take US 70A. Stay straight to head onto US 79. (US 79 becomes US 79/TN 76.) Turn left onto US 641/TN 69 north. Turn left onto TN 54/TN 69, and drive straight into Paris. It's worth mentioning that Paris is within a day's drive of 74 percent of the nation's population and has been recognized as part of the fastest-growing recreational area in the nation. Paris became the seat of Henry County on September 23, 1823. It remains the oldest incorporated municipality. During the Civil War, Henry County was named the "Volunteer County of the Volunteer State" for sending more than 2,500 volunteers to the Confederacy. And during World War II, a camp was erected right outside Paris to train servicemen and to house German prisoners of war. The town gained its name in honor of the French town as a way of paying tribute to General Lafayette, who visited Tennessee in the early 1800s.

WHERE TO GO

Henry County Chamber of Commerce. 2508 East Wood Street, Paris, TN 38242. There's a lot of history behind the town of Paris, so

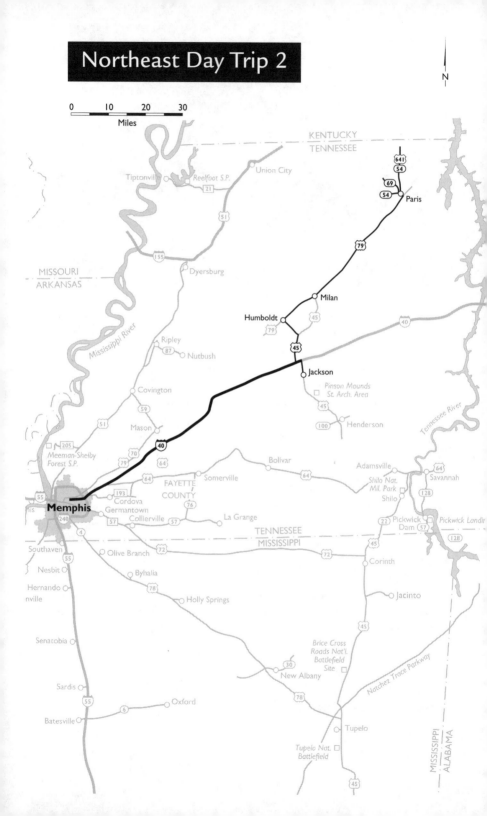

Northeast Day Trip 2

stop in the chamber of commerce to pick up some brochures that describe the town's roots and its attractions. (731) 642-3431.

Paris Revisited Tour. 2508 East Wood Street, Paris, TN 38242. This walking tour leads you through the streets of West Tennessee's oldest incorporated community. Guided by a historical audiotape narrative, you're led through downtown Paris, the North Poplar Street Historic District, and the Old City Cemetery—each listed on the National Register of Historic Places. Along the way you'll pass five historic churches, which are known for their beautiful stained-glass windows. Free. (731) 642-3431.

Paris–Henry County Heritage Center. 614 Poplar Street, Paris, TN 38242. Visitors are encouraged to walk through this extraordinary Italianate mansion, referred to as "a crown jewel of Paris." It serves the community as a museum, archives, and research and education center. The mansion was built by philanthropist Colonel Barton and named Cavitt Place. To date, its marble staircase and floors, mahogany woodwork, and stained glass have all been preserved. Many of the wall paintings remain intact as well. (731) 642-1030.

Paris Landing State Park. 16055 Highway 79 North, Buchanan, TN 38222. Just east of the Paris city limits lies Paris Landing State Park. Named for a steamboat and freight landing, the area served in the mid-1800s as a place where supplies were exchanged for transport to surrounding communities. The 841-acre park sits on the edge of Kentucky Lake, one of the largest man-made lakes in the world. In addition to fishing, the park is also a great location for boating and hiking. If you choose to bring a boat, you'll be interested to learn that the park has just installed a new service dock with fuel and supplies, as well as a free launch ramp surrounded by plenty of parking. Paris Landing State Park also has one of West Tennessee's finest eighteen-hole golf courses, as well as tennis courts and an archery range. (731) 644-7359.

Fort Donelson National Battlefield and Cemetery. 1337 Donelson, Dover, TN 37058. The cemetery was chartered in 1867 and serves as the resting place for Union soldiers killed at Fort Donelson, as well as area veterans who died in all of the seven major wars. Begin your visit with a stop at the visitor center to get a map of the grounds, which include the Dover Hotel and Fort Donelson. The Dover Hotel, which is also referred to as Surrender House, was the location where Confederate general Simon Buckner surrendered to

Ulysses S. Grant. You can also tour Fort Donelson's earthen rifle pits and river batteries. (931) 232-8511.

Clarksville Speedway. 1600 Needmore Road, Clarksville, TN 37040. Known by frequent visitors as a place to see "Southern dirt track racing at its best," the speedway is the best way to get in the action and watch stock-car drivers race to the finish line. Every Saturday night you can see the "Rolling Thunder" live at the speedway. The track is 0.25 mile long and made of high banked clay. You'll also find UMP late models, modifieds, pro streets, street stocks, and mini stocks. (931) 645-2523.

WHERE TO SHOP

Antiques shops. Scavenging old stores for even older finds is sheer pleasure for antiquers. And in Paris, Tennessee, there are some great shops to choose from, many within walking distance of one another. Wander through these popular spots and browse the booths for silver, crystal, linens, furniture, and collectibles. Because the merchandise changes regularly, you never know what wonderful treasures lie ahead at each of these uncommon shops. One thing is for certain: Given the wide array of antiques stores in this town, you're sure to leave with something.

Antiques on the Square. 118 West Washington Street, Paris, TN 38242. (731) 644-2090.

G&G's Flea Market and Antiques. 1419 North Market Street, Paris, TN 38242. (731) 641-0009.

Grapevine Mall. 114 West Washington Street, Paris, TN 38242. (731) 642-7850.

Market Street Antique Mall. 414 North Market Street, Paris, TN 38242. (731) 642-6996.

Old Depot Antique Mall. 203 North Fentress Street, Paris, TN 38242. (731) 642-0222.

WHERE TO STAY

Riverfront Plantation Inn B&B. 190 Crow Lane, Dover, TN 37058. Perched overlooking the peaceful Cumberland River, the Riverfront Plantation Inn is a majestic sight. This pre-Civil War plantation has been beautifully restored. It's conveniently located next to the Fort Donelson National Battlefield, and the property and surrounding lands are luscious and sprawling. The inn features five luxurious rooms, each named for a famous figure such as Robert E. Lee, Nathan Bedford Forrest, or Stonewall Jackson. In the dining room choose from selections of beef, seafood, buffalo, chicken, and pork; the mushroom-stuffed beef tenderloin and coconut shrimp are house favorites. Every morning coffee, pastries, and juice are brought to your room to help you start your day. Then you can head to the dining room at your convenience to enjoy a full plantation breakfast. $$-$$$; □. (931) 232-9492.

Oak Haven Resort. 248 Oak Haven Road, Buchanan, TN 38222. The Oak Haven Resort has been in business for more than fifteen years and makes one promise—to provide you with peace and quiet (along with lots of fun) for the entire family. Their motto is, "We treat you like part of our family." The resort sits on eight acres overlooking Eagle Bay and has full trailer hookups as well as cottages and direct access to Kentucky Lake. Look for square- and round-dancing clubs as well as many other summer and fall activities. The family-size apartments include a living room, kitchen, bedrooms, and bathroom. $$; □. (731) 642-1550.

SPECIAL EVENTS

World's Biggest Fish Fry. April. Each year more than 100,000 visitors pour into Paris, Tennessee, to witness and participate in the World's Biggest Fish Fry. For a small charge, you can help yourself to as much catfish and fixin's as you can eat. Activities include cooking, a parade, a rodeo, a car show, a carnival, and arts and crafts. (731) 642-3431.

Freedom Festival. July. Annually, visitors gather at the nearby town of Cottage Grove to celebrate their American heritage. The wide range of activities includes a parade, carnival, turkey shoot, music, dancing, fireworks, and a barbecue. (731) 782-3692.

Eiffel Tower Day. September. Eiffel Tower Day takes place in Memorial Park, and includes balloon races, arts and crafts, food, games, and live entertainment. The name pays tribute to the other well-known city of Paris. (731) 642-3431.

Annual Storytelling Festival. September. The Storytelling Festival is held every year at Ogburn Park, where professional storytellers gather to spin tales and provide entertainment for guests of all ages.

Cordova, TN; Germantown, TN; Collierville, TN

CORDOVA

If you live in Memphis, you've probably been to Cordova, but maybe you didn't know it. It's a twenty-minute drive on I–40 east (get off at Germantown Road) to Wolfchase Galleria, the premier shopping center in the metro-Memphis area. Cordova is also home to a rapidly increasing population. Its close proximity to Memphis and its freshness all contribute to making it a superb little enclave not just to live in but also to visit for the day. When you exit the interstate at Germantown Road, Cordova is primarily on the south side of the road. To the north are both the Galleria and several strip malls flanked by chain restaurants. But to the south you'll find the heart of Cordova: shops and restaurants covering the street, with newly developed subdivisions just behind.

WHERE TO GO

Cordova Cellars Winery. 9050 Macon Road, Cordova, TN 38018. Founded in the late 1980s, the young but prosperous Cordova Cellars has four and a half acres of chardonnay and vidal vines. The ample and fertile vines produce enough grapes for 5,000 gallons of wine each year. That's about 2,000 cases, or 24,000 bottles. In 1993 Gault-Millan, which publishes a fine dining, hotel, and wine guidebook, named Cordova Cellars one of the best wineries of North America. The winery is open daily for tours and on most weekends hosts concerts and other special events. Visitors bring picnic baskets

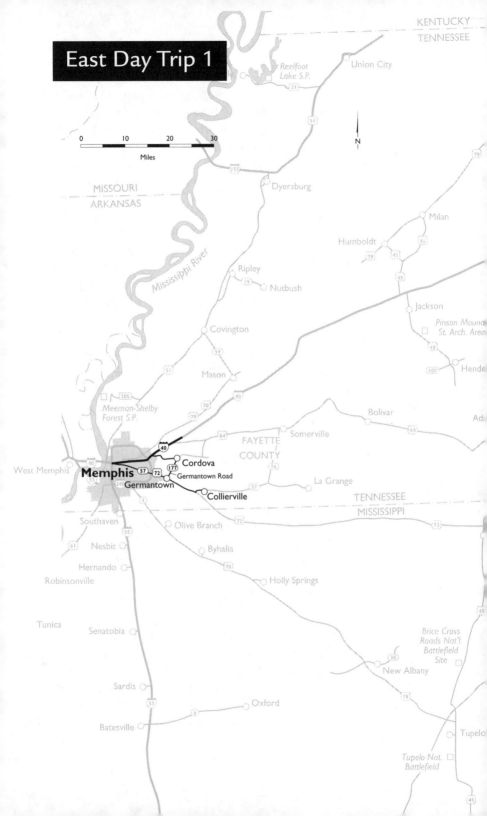

East Day Trip 1

MISSISSIPPI RIVER

KENTUCKY
TENNESSEE

Union City

Reelfoot
Lake S.P.

21

0   10   20   30
Miles

N

MISSOURI
ARKANSAS

Dyersburg

Milan

Humboldt

79   45   45

Ripley

Nutbush

Jackson

Pinson Mound
St. Arch. Area

Covington

59

43

Mason

100   Hende

51

70   40

Meeman-Shelby
Forest S.P.

205

79

Bolivar

Ad

64

Somerville

FAYETTE
COUNTY

64

West Memphis

40

Memphis   57   72

55

24

4

40

Cordova
177

Germantown Road

Germantown

76

La Grange

57

Collierville

TENNESSEE
MISSISSIPPI

Southaven

55

72

Olive Branch

72

Nesbit

61

Byhalia

Hernando

78

Robinsonville

Holly Springs

45

Tunica

Senatobia

Brice Cross
Roads Nat'l.
Battlefield
Site

New Albany

30

Sardis

78

55

Oxford

Batesville

6

Tupelo Nat.
Battlefield

Tupelo

45

filled with gourmet take-out and spread out on a blanket to enjoy the outdoor entertainment along with their Cordova wine, which includes chardonnay, blushing venus, white on white, merlot, and even apple cider. Every once in a while, the winery hosts a Winemaker's Dinner. If you have any questions, call your host Randy Birks; he'll fill you in on what's coming up. Open Tuesday through Sunday. (901) 754-3442.

Cordova Skating Center. 7970 Club Drive, Cordova, TN 38018. For those of you who haven't roller skated in twenty years, the Cordova Skating Center may sound a little intimidating—kids whizzing by, strobe lights flashing. But imagine how much fun you and a skating partner would have reliving your youth. And if you have children of your own, the skating rink makes a great family outing. You can rent skates and grab the standard "attraction" fare at the snack bar. If you're lucky and the DJ's feeling especially groovy, he'll take requests for your favorite tunes to boogie skate. Open afternoons on the weekend; call ahead for weekday hours. (901) 755-0221.

Bogey's Golf and Family Entertainment Center. 7800 Fischer Steel Road, Cordova, TN 38018. Nothing beats miniature golf for a relaxing outdoor activity, and Bogey's Golf is one of the best miniature courses in the Memphis area. But Bogey's isn't just for golf balls: There's also go-carts, an arcade, a driving range, and so many kiddie rides that you'll never hear the end of it. Go at night to add a little fun to a romantic evening; go during the afternoon with friends for a little lively competition; or take the kids for some serious amateur golfing. Bring your own snacks or partake of Bogey's own concessions for only a few bucks. (901) 757-2649.

WHERE TO SHOP

Wolfchase Galleria. 2760 North Germantown Parkway, Memphis, TN 38133. Technically speaking, Wolfchase Galleria is in a Memphis zip code, but it's smack dab in the middle of Bartlett and Cordova. Developers couldn't make up their minds, so Memphis claimed the mall. As you exit the interstate, you'll be right where Bartlett and Cordova sort of melt into each other, divided only by the overpass. So if you're in Cordova, just pop over the I-40 bridge and you'll find yourself surrounded by *Retail*. The Galleria is on the right (east) side of Germantown Parkway and houses such familiar stores as Pottery Barn, Ann Taylor, Gymboree, and Goldsmiths. It's definitely the upscale answer to Memphis's shopping woes. If children are in tow, take them to the mall's center, where they'll be enamored with a gloriously colorful and musical carousel. When you set your eyes on it, chances are you'll want to take a turn yourself. (901) 372-9409.

The Belz Factory Outlets. 3536 Canada Road, Lakeland, TN 38002. Just a jog farther down I-40 is the Canada Road exit, where you'll turn off to the south and find the outlets on your left. There are two separate buildings, so be sure not to stop after the first one, which boasts the Nike outlet. In the second building, which is like an indoor mall, make a beeline to Oldtime Pottery. It's a massive, filled-to-capacity craft store, a la Michaels—but bigger, better, and cheaper. You'll find dishes and stemware, picture frames, candles, silk and dried flowers, vases, posters, prints... the list goes on and on. Oldtime is a must-stop for any holiday paraphernalia: hearts for Valentine's Day, clovers for St. Pat's, flags for the Fourth of July, ceramic pumpkins for Halloween, harvest items for Thanksgiving, wreaths for Christmas, and sparklers and hats for New Year's. By shopping at the Belz Factory Outlets, you're supporting a Memphis native: The Belz family still lives here. For information about the outlet center, call the management office. (901) 386-3180.

WHERE TO EAT

There are so many places to eat in Cordova that if you just drive a few blocks, you're sure to find something, but most of the restaurants in this suburban setting are well-known chain spots. If you want what you know, stop anywhere along Germantown Road for a wide variety: Red Lobster, Chili's, Huey's (a Memphis favorite), Appleby's. But if you're looking for something a little different, try one of the restaurants below.

EJ's Brasserie. 1848 North Germantown Parkway, Cordova, TN 38013. EJ's is Erling Jensen's baby. If you're familiar with Memphis fine dining, you're familiar with Erling, and you're familiar with his special blend of Dutch and French haute cuisine. EJ's Brasserie is the more casual, more bustling of Erling's restaurants, which have been a Memphis stronghold for years. The brasserie's decor is classic Parisian, while its menu is nouveau Dutch with a little French zest in keeping with the brasserie ambience. $$$; ☐. (901) 751-1150.

Bahama Breeze. 2830 North Germantown Parkway, Memphis, TN 38133. If you've found Wolfchase, you can't miss Bahama Breeze. This hip and happening restaurant—hippest at night—is smack in front of the mall, right on the corner of Germantown Parkway and Stage Road (hence the Memphis address). One reason Bahama Breeze is such a rave at night is the wide selection of "island" drinks offered—mango daiquiris are a favorite. Another sundown draw is the crackling fire kept going on the patio. You can grab a drink at the outdoor bar and settle down at a fireside table or bench to feel the cozy warmth on a cool spring night. If you're ready for a meal, wander inside, where you'll find a fiestalike atmosphere and a terrific range of eclectic island food. Seafood prevails, but steaks and pasta are available in equally interesting combinations. Some particularly tasty dishes are spicy flame-grilled fresh tilapia, the jerk pork chop, coconut curry chicken, Bahamian kabobs, and steak con mojo. $$; ☐. (901) 385-8744.

WHERE TO STAY

Bridgewater House Bed and Breakfast. 7015 Raleigh LaGrange Road, Cordova, TN 38018. If you go to the Bridgewater House, you'll be escaping both Memphis and the twenty-first century. Built in 1890 as a schoolhouse, this Greek Revival–style bed-and-breakfast is filled with antiques, travel memorabilia, and heirlooms. The two bedrooms each offer private bath and luxury linens. When you arrive, you'll be treated to afternoon or early-evening refreshments. In the warmer months guests enjoy playing croquet on the grounds and lounging on the patio; during colder months everyone relaxes around the fireplace to read or play cards. The owners, Steve and Katherine Mistilis, have culinary backgrounds and treat guests to a multicourse gourmet breakfast. They'll also prepare a custom lunch or dinner for special occasions. The Bridgewater offers stay and dining packages, so call ahead for information. $$; ☐. (901) 384-0080; (800) 466-1001.

GERMANTOWN

From I–40 and Cordova, drive south along Germantown Road. It'll take you about fifteen minutes to reach Germantown proper. As you emerge onto Poplar Avenue—which, incidentally, you can take to get there from midtown—you'll find once again a haven of retail shopping. But Germantown, which has a longer history than its northern counterpart Cordova, has a little more charm and a little less glamour. Just west of Germantown Road on Poplar, you'll run into Saddle Creek, a leisurely outdoor shopping mall where moms stroll with their kids and business workers meet at the bistros and cafes for lunch. Although Germantown—named for its early German immigrant settlers—was incorporated in the mid-1800s and considered itself "horse country" until about fifty years ago, this suburb of metro Memphis is now the fifteenth largest city in Tennessee. Germantown residents have maintained their community's history and interest in horses by hosting the annual Germantown Charity Horse Show, which is a huge Memphis tradition.

WHERE TO GO

Germantown Chamber of Commerce. 2195 Germantown Road South, Germantown, TN 38138. The chamber can provide you with brochures on the area and answer your questions about attractions and businesses. Open Monday through Friday. (901) 755-1200.

    Fort Germantown. 3085 Honey Tree Drive, Germantown, TN 38138. Fort Germantown is listed on the National Register of Historic Places and is marked by replicas of Howitzer cannons. It was here, during the Civil War, that 250 Union troops constructed an earthwork redoubt to serve as a fort guarding the Memphis & Charleston Railroad. (901) 755-1200.

    Oaklawn Gardens. 7831 Old Poplar Pike, Germantown, TN 38138. Oaklawn Gardens is located on the grounds of the home of Harry and Becky Cloyes. Here you'll find a collection of Germantown historical artifacts, including the town's first fire truck and the cagelike cell that served as the first city jail. (901) 755-1200.

Germantown Depot. 2260 West Street, Germantown, TN 38138. The Germantown Depot is located near the original city hall at Germantown Road and the Norfolk & Southern Railroad tracks, smack in the center of the Old Germantown District. The depot, built in 1868, was originally a stop along the Memphis & Charleston Railroad's southern lines and now houses an exhibit of railroad memorabilia. It was rebuilt in 1948. Check it out if you are interested in trains or metro–Memphis history. (901) 755-1200.

Germantown Performing Arts Centre. 1801 Exeter Road, Germantown, TN 38138. GPAC, as it's known locally, is a first-class performing arts facility. In addition to its annual series of concerts—classical, jazz, Broadway—the Germantown Performing Arts Centre hosts a number of educational programs, largely geared toward children ages five through eighteen, in the areas of dance, theater, and music. The conductor of the Germantown Symphony, Michael Stern, attracts such famous musicians as YoYo Ma. Be sure to check GPAC's calendar of events to schedule your day—or night—trip. Tickets to the concerts range from $12 to $50. ☐. www.gpacweb.com/. (901) 757-7256.

WHERE TO SHOP

Saddle Creek. Northeast corner of Poplar Avenue and West Street, Germantown, TN 38138. It's hard to imagine a classier shopping center than Saddle Creek. A brick terrace, complete with arched doorways and a fountain, makes up its walkway, which guides you into such stores as Williams Sonoma, Origins, Nicole Miller, Banana Republic, J. Crew, and Crabtree & Evelyn. This is where the sophisticated people shop. But Saddle Creek also appeals to the younger crowds with flashy and hip boutiques like Indigo, where buyers indulge in platform shoes and flared jeans. Probably the best thing about this upscale "strip mall" is the window-shopping. Shopkeepers take special care in creating pretty-as-a-picture displays in the framed glass of their stores. For more information, call the management office. (901) 761-2571.

WHERE TO EAT

Yia Yia's. 7615 West Farmington, Germantown, TN 38138. Once a beleaguered Ruby Tuesdays, this spot is now the very happening and very eclectic Yia Yia's, named after the Greek owner's grandmother. Everything goes at Yia Yia's: wood-oven pizza, Mediterranean salads, hearty tenderloin, spicy seafood, and far-out pastas, which can be ordered in full or half portions. The theme is bistro, but the menu is a blend of Greek, Turkish, Lebanese, and Italian influences. The bartender will pour you a solid eight-ounce glass of wine or mix up a house specialty, like the Bellini or Mother's Milk Margarita (with homemade margarita mix). To avoid the typical hour-plus wait for a table, call ahead and the hostess will put you on "the list." $$–$$$; ☐. (901) 756-4004.

Bosco's. 7615 West Farmington, Suite 30, Germantown, TN 38138. It doesn't get more "Germantown" than Bosco's, which occupies the space just next to the north fountain at Saddle Creek. Bosco's has breezy and relaxing patio seating, but the real selling point is its famous home-brewed beer. The most popular flavor is Germantown Alt, which has won numerous national beer contests. In addition, Bosco's brews select "regulars" and a variety of seasonal beers, including a pumpkin beer in fall. There's also an entire menu of pizzas, pastas, and meat dishes waiting for you. If no one is sitting in the Tom Cruise booth—where the actor sat for a scene in *The Firm*—ask for it, and read the clip framed at the table for a little taste of Hollywood to go with your Alt. $$; ☐. www.boscosbeer.com. (901) 756-7310.

The Marble Slab. 7615 West Farmington, Germantown, TN 38138. After dinner at Bosco's or Yia Yia's, you can take a stroll through Saddle Creek to the best new ice cream joint in the metro-Memphis area: the Marble Slab. It's so good and so refreshing that the "Slab" has become a bit of a hangout. Patrons get to pick out their ice cream flavor and "topping" before watching the clerk smash it all together on a marble slab—hence, the name. $. (901) 759-9052.

The Germantown Commissary. 2290 South Germantown Road, Germantown, TN 38138. Some say Rendez-Vous is Memphis's best barbecue, but die-hards still go to Germantown Commissary to get their pork. It's easy to miss, so you have to be looking for it (on your left) as you cross the railroad tracks and make your way into German-town's Old District. Most people get Commissary take-out, because there's not much room to sit down and stretch out after putting back a rack of ribs or a giant pork plate. But if you can't wait until you get home, you certainly can park yourself at one of the Commissary picnic tables to enjoy your meal. $–$$; ☐. (901) 754-5540.

Three Oaks Grill. 2285 South Germantown Road, Germantown, TN 38138. With so many places to eat in Germantown, it's hard for one to stand out, but Three Oaks has managed to make a name for itself with its cozy but expansive main dining room and nouveau French menu. It's a sister restaurant to Paulette's in midtown Memphis, but Three Oaks departs from the midtown brasserie with its majestic decor: huge vaulted and timbered ceilings, a grand fireplace, and an entire wall of glass doors that open onto Old Germantown Road. The menu includes the popular shrimp with sausage gravy, a truly tender tenderloin, and a changing seafood special. $$$; ☐. (901) 757-8225.

SPECIAL EVENTS

Germantown Charity Horse Show. June. The Charity Horse Show is one of Germantown's claims to fame. It lasts for five days in June and was first held in 1948. It hosts nearly 1,000 horses each year and is one of the largest multibreed horse shows in the country. (901) 754-7443.

Fourth of July Family Celebration. July 4. One of the biggest Fourth of July events in the metro area, the Germantown Family Celebration hosts activities for all ages, along with fireworks and an outdoor concert. Take your family and your picnic down to Municipal Park for a blast. (901) 757-7376.

Germantown Festival. September. Every year on the first weekend after Labor Day, Germantown sponsors the festival for two days at C. O. Franklin Park. You'll find the standard festival fare: arts, crafts, food, music, and activities for the whole family. (901) 757-9212.

FedEx–St. Jude Classic Golf Tournament. Summer. The FESJC has become one of the PGA Tour's major southern tournaments. It's held at Southwind's Tournament Players Club to benefit St. Jude Children's Research Hospital. The PGA determines the dates each year, so call ahead. (901) 748-0534.

COLLIERVILLE

To finish off your day trip through metro Memphis, get back onto Poplar Avenue, also known as US 72, and head east. After a ten-minute drive, turn right onto North Main Street, which will take you right into Collierville's historic town square. There you'll find everything you need for an afternoon of browsing, sipping, eating, and playing. If you drive just a little farther, you can even ride. Horses, that is. At last count, there were seven riding stables in Collierville: It's definitely horse country.

Technically, Collierville has been around for more than a hundred years, but only in the last decade has it really become a major draw for Memphis. In 2000 FedEx moved its international corporate headquarters to a Collierville, boosting the city's recognition and economy. Now Collierville is not just a little burb east of Memphis but a prospering, historic city in its own right, with residents who show great pride in and dedication to maintaining the intimate, yet increasingly cosmopolitan, atmosphere. The nonprofit group Main Street Collierville, which seeks to maintain the history of the city, headlines its Web site with a statement that sums up the general attitude not just of the group itself but of all the people who live in town: "Main Street Collierville believes that if a community preserves the integrity of its heritage, that heritage will, in turn, preserve the integrity of the community." To celebrate and maintain Collierville's history, city leaders are continually organizing and sponsoring such things as community events, architectural revivals, and historical exhibits. So though you won't find many museums or monuments to visit, you will find an ongoing and varied list of events to plan your trip around.

WHERE TO GO

Collierville Chamber of Commerce. 215 South Center Street, Collierville, TN 38017. The chamber can provide visitors with maps and information about the area. Open weekdays. www.collierville.com. (901) 853-1949.

Historic town square. 111 Walnut Street (downtown), Collierville, TN 38017. Collierville's town square has a unique plan—historic commercial buildings on three sides and the depot and railroad on the fourth. There's Confederate Park and a bandstand, along with turn-of-the-twentieth-century walkways laid out in the form of a Confederate flag, cast-iron fences, and an old-fashioned clock. On the south side of the square rests the stagecoach. During the second half of the nineteenth century, Collierville residents used this log cabin as their stagecoach stop. It was originally built in 1851 by William Talley in another location and moved here in 1977. The entire square is a great place to stroll, or—as they used to say—promenade. Contact Main Street Collierville, a nonprofit organization dedicated to preserving this spot, for more information about both the square and other historic areas. (901) 853-1666.

The depot. Town Square, Collierville, TN. In October 1863 General Sherman's train arrived from Memphis at this depot, believed to have been located on the north side of the railroad tracks between Center and Walnut Streets. Although there's no museum or tour here, the depot offers you a chance to see a significant historic landmark: the site of the battle of Collierville. Another depot was located where Center Street crosses the railroad tracks. The existing depot was moved in the 1940s from La Grange, then moved again to its current location in 1977. (901) 853-1666.

Heritage Railroad and Memphis Transportation Museum. 125 North Rowlett, Collierville, TN 38017. Located near the depot, this train display is basically a collection of historically significant train cars, including a 1912 steam engine built for the Frisco Railroad; a 1915 executive's car called the Savannah with a nearly intact interior; a 1920s caboose; and several cars from the 1930s and '40s. During World War II steam engine number 1351 pulled troop trains. Contact Pat Plemmons at (901) 683-2266 or Main Street Collierville at (901) 853-1666 for more information.

W. C. Johnson Park. Wolf River Drive and Johnson Park Drive, Collierville, TN 38017. The 135-acre W. C. Johnson Park is located along 75 acres of wetlands, which occupy the Wolf River Corridor. This is also where the multiphase Peterson Lake Nature Center is being built. Portions of this nature project are already open to the public, including a 1.5-mile boardwalk in the wetlands and a tranquil observation area overlooking Peterson Lake and the surrounding natural environment of the Wolf River. Call Collierville Community Center for Parks, Recreation, and Cultural Arts for more information. (901) 853-3225.

Horseback riding and stables. Nothing beats getting out of the city for a little history, a splash of nature, and a long ride on a beast of burden. But there's nothing burdensome about Collierville's horses: They'll prance you around and take you over hill and dale until sundown. You'll come home a little sore but feeling earthy and relaxed. There are half a dozen or more riding stables in Collierville. Here are three to try:

Meadow Wood Stable. 10455 Raleigh LaGrange Road, Collierville, TN 38017. (901) 853-1945.

Shady Creek Farm. 11083 Shady Lane, Collierville, TN 38017. (901) 854-0040.

M & M Stables. 9841 Holmes Road, Collierville, TN 38017. (901) 854-4007.

WHERE TO SHOP

Antiques shops. Collierville, especially its town square, is home to more than a dozen antiques shops, which sell everything from eighteenth century English furnishings to early-twentieth-century art. Here are a few favorites:

Town Square Antique Mall. 118 East Mulberry Street, Collierville, TN 38017. (901) 854-9839.

English Country Antiques. 102 East Mulberry Street, Collierville, TN 38017. (901) 853-3170.

White Church Antiques & Tea Room. 196 North Main Street, Collierville, TN 38017. (901) 854-6433.

Liberty Tree Antiques. 120 North Main Street, Collierville, TN 38017. (901) 854-4364.

WHERE TO EAT

Café on the Square. 120 West Mulberry Street, Collierville, TN 38017. This cafe, convenient to your exploration of the historic town square, offers sandwiches, salads, grilled dishes, and a variety of sides. What's most interesting about Café on the Square, though, is the history of its building. It was originally constructed as a drugstore, circa 1900; Tom Ruch, the manager, lived with his family in the back of the store. $-$$; ☐. (901) 853-7511.

Silver Caboose Restaurant & Soda Fountain. 132 East Mulberry Street, Collierville, TN 38017. It's the real deal: an authentic soda fountain. In addition, the Silver Caboose Restaurant and Soda Fountain offers diners food "homemade from scratch, using treasured grandmother's recipes." It's a casual dining experience with a full-service bar right on the historic Collierville town square. The building itself was constructed in 1890. During the

1920s it served as Biggs and Dudney Grocery Store. $$; □. (901) 853-0010.

SPECIAL EVENTS

Fair on the Square. May. Fair on the Square began in 1976 to celebrate the American Bicentennial. It was such a success that the Twentieth Century Club, the event's sponsor, has kept the tradition alive. At the fair, townspeople and visitors can indulge in a wide variety of foods and activities for the whole family. Mark your calendar for the first weekend in May. (901) 853-6228.

Sunset on the Square. June–July. Every Thursday night at 7:00 P.M. during June and July, locals and nonlocals alike flock—with lawn chairs and picnic baskets in tow—to the center of town for the Sunset on the Square concert series. Music ranges from bluegrass to classical to Broadway. The best part is that it's free. (901) 853-1666.

Partners in Preservation. August. The "Preservation Party" is an annual event and one of the mainstays of Collierville, as it raises the funds necessary to keep the town's heritage alive. Partygoers sample food from more than twenty area restaurants and dance to music provided by live bands. The focus of the evening is the silent auction, with many big-ticket items donated by local merchants. (901) 853-1666.

Dickens on the Square. Early December. Dickens on the Square is a holiday festival typically held the first weekend of December. It's an outdoor event with music, theater, a marketplace, Victorian characters, carriage rides, food, and children's activities. To top off the event, Charles Dickens's great-great-grandson Gerald Charles Dickens makes a special appearance. (901) 853-1666.

Santa Express. December. At Christmastime, the square looks like a twinkling wonderland and hosts the Santa Express, where children can have their picture taken with Santa atop a vintage train car. (901) 853-6777.

CORINTH

Poplar Avenue takes you all the way to Corinth—really. It just changes names a few times. From Memphis, head east on Poplar, go through Collierville, and keep going as Poplar becomes US 72. Then turn right onto MS 45. Corinth is nestled right in the intersection of these highways. It takes almost two hours to get there. If you're a Civil War buff, Corinth is an absolute must. When Brigadier General Ulysses S. Grant said to his men, "There will be no fighting at Pittsburgh Landing; we will have to go to Corinth," he put this small Mississippi town into the history books forever. It was from Corinth that the armies set out for the battle of Shiloh in the early days of April 1862. Both the Corinth battle site and the local Civil War locations are considered National Historic Landmarks.

WHERE TO GO

Corinth Area Tourism and Promotion Council. 602 East Waldron Street, Corinth, MS 38834. Stop in the tourism office to get a handful of maps and brochures on the area. The council also maintains a great Web site: www.corinth.net. Open weekdays. (662) 287-8300; (800) 748-9048.

Northeast Mississippi Museum. 204 East Fourth Street, Corinth, MS 38834. You can indulge in all the Civil War and American Indian history surrounding Corinth by visiting the Northeast Mississippi Museum, located at Fourth and Washington Streets. The

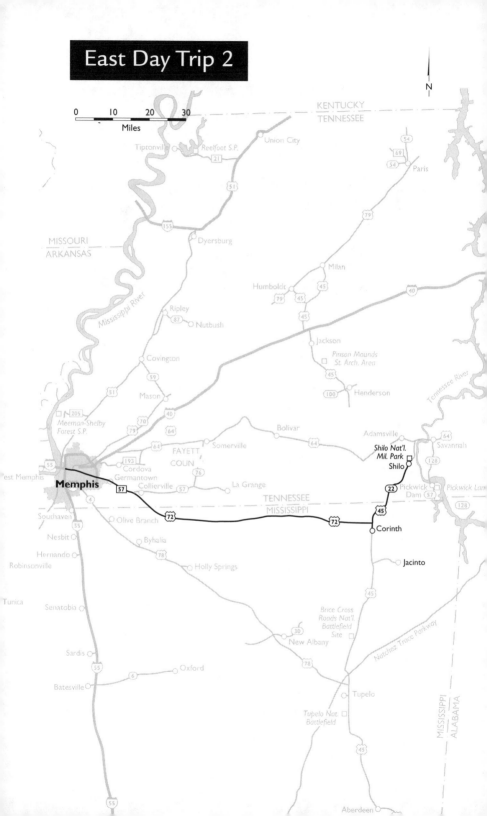

East Day Trip 2

0   10   20   30
Miles

KENTUCKY
TENNESSEE

Tiptonville   Reelfoot S.P.   Union City   54

69
54   Paris

21

51

155

MISSOURI
ARKANSAS   Dyersburg   79

Milan

Humboldt   45   10
79   45

Ripley   45

Nutbush   87

Jackson   Pinson Mounds
St. Arch. Area

Covington   45

59   100   Henderson

Mason   51

205
Meeman-Shelby   70   40   64   Bolivar   Adamsville   64
Forest S.P.   79   64   Somerville   64   Shilo Nat'l.   Savannah
Mil. Park   128
West Memphis   55   FAYETT   Shilo
COUN
193   76   22   Pickwick
Cordova   Dam   57   Pickwick Lan
Germantown   22
Memphis   Collierville   57   La Grange   TENNESSEE   45   128
57   MISSISSIPPI
4   72   72   Corinth
Southaven   Olive Branch   72
55
Nesbit   Byhalia   Jacinto
Hernando   78
Robinsonville   Holly Springs   45

Tunica   Senatobia   Brice Cross
Roads Nat'l.
Battlefield
Site
Sardis   30
New Albany   Natchez Trace Parkway

Oxford   78
55
6
Batesville   Tupelo

MISSISSIPPI
ALABAMA

Tupelo Nat.
Battlefield

45

55   Aberdeen

museum has a fine collection of Civil War and Chickasaw Indian artifacts, as well as other exhibits, and museum guides will take you on a tour. If you're a true Civil War buff, stop into the research room, where a multitude of records is available for your perusal. In addition to diaries and letters from the war, the research room houses a vast collection of genealogical material. If your family tree branches out into Mississippi, chances are you'll be able to track down those ancestors here. Free. (662) 287-3120.

Curlee House. 301 Childs Street, Corinth, MS 38834. One of sixteen places in Corinth on the National Register of Historic Places, the Curlee House is a Greek Revival mansion built in 1857. Its grand windows, high ceilings, iron moulding, and period furnishings take you right back to the days when three Civil War generals lived there. Braxton Bragg and Earl Van Dorn of the Confederate army stayed here around 1862, once their forces had retreated south. Later, Union general Henry Halleck turned the house into his temporary headquarters. Eventually the Curlee House was returned to its owners. Today, visitors can tour the home and grounds every afternoon, except holidays. Fee. (662) 287-9501.

Civil War Visitors Center at the Curlee House. 301 Childs Street, Corinth, MS 38834. This Civil War interpretive center borders the property of the Curlee House and is under the same management. The center provides information about Civil War history pertaining especially to the northeastern Mississippi area. Visitors may view a twelve-minute video of the siege and battle of Corinth and begin their walking and driving tour of the campaign for Corinth from its front door. Both the center and the Curlee are open year-round, every day of the week. Free with admission to Curlee House. (662) 287-9501.

Jacinto Courthouse. County Road 367, Jacinto, MS 38834. The Jacinto Courthouse—one of the South's premier examples of federal style architecture—is a fifteen-minute drive south from Corinth. Take US 45 south and turn east onto MS 356, which will then take you into Jacinto where you'll pick up County Road 367. The courthouse was built in 1852 and served as the seat for Tishomingo County. There's a park area and walking trails for recreation. The courthouse is also the site of the Jacinto Fourth of July Festival (see Special Events). Contact Betsy Whitehurst for more information. Free. (662) 286-8662.

Battery Robinett. Linden Street, Corinth, MS 38834. To complete your tour of Civil War Corinth, head out to Battery Robinett, which was built by the federal army as an artillery battery. Robinett is the future site of a planned $9-million Civil War interpretive center, scheduled to open in 2003. Free. (662) 287–8300; (800) 748–9048.

WHERE TO SHOP

Corinth Flea Market. 1224 Highway 72 East, Corinth, MS 38834. The flea market is located in the Corinth Square Shopping Center. It's open Wednesday through Sunday and has standard flea market fare. (601) 287–1387; (601) 287–9110.

WHERE TO EAT

Borroum's Drug and Soda Fountain. 604 East Waldron Street, Corinth, MS 38834. This is the real McCoy. Borroum's doesn't even have a canned soda in the vicinity of its old-fashioned soda fountain. In addition to a fountain drink, you can partake in a Corinth town special: the slugburger (see Special Events for the Slugburger Festival), which was made from soy and cornmeal during World War II meat rationing. The burger is named for the "slug"—or nickel— because that's how much it cost way back then. Borroum's main claim to fame, though, is its designation as the oldest family-owned drugstore in the state of Mississippi. It was opened in 1865 by Dr. Borroum, a surgeon with the Confederate army, and is still in the family today. $–$$. (662) 286–3361.

WHERE TO STAY

General's Quarters Bed and Breakfast Inn. 924 Fillmore Street, Corinth, MS 38834. Charlotte and Luke Doehner, along with their two dogs and cat, will welcome you warmly to their newly expanded Victorian inn, built in 1872. In response to great demand, the Doehners recently added six rooms, bringing the total to ten. Each of the guest rooms has a private bath; the suite offers a nineteenth-century canopy bed. Perhaps the best thing about General's Quarters is the upstairs parlor and porch, which allows guests to mingle together or to enjoy a good book or game of cards. Breakfast is served in the formal dining room with an ample dose of southern hospitality. Included in your room rate is an early-evening cocktail. The inn also offers a garden hot tub, a gift shop, a full library, and a beautiful garden area. $$; ☐. (662) 286-3325.

Bed and Breakfast at Robbin's Nest. 1523 Shiloh Road, Corinth, MS 38834. Everyone who stays at the Robbin's Nest, a Southern Colonial-style inn with magnificent front columns, says it's "dripping with charm." Anne, a Corinth native, and Tony Whyte have created a traditional bed-and-breakfast with antiques and a cozy atmosphere. There are three bedrooms, all with queen-size beds and private bath. This historic building, on land shaded by magnolias, overlooks a gorgeous garden area in back, which you can enjoy from an old-fashioned wicker lounge chair on the patio as you sip an authentic mint julep. The B&B is a convenient spot from which to explore the Civil War attractions nearby. $$; ☐. (662) 286-3109.

Ravenswood Bed and Breakfast. 1002 Douglas Street, Corinth, MS 38834. Built in 1929 and cited on Civil War earthworks, Ravenswood is an arts-and-crafts home. Ron Wayne Smith and Timothy Hodges own the B&B and maintain the relaxing, casual atmosphere that guests love. The inn is located on one and a half wooded acres, near many of the historic northeast Mississippi landmarks. Your hosts will direct you on a true "Civil War" journey, taking you back to 1862, with walking and driving tours. Three rooms have private baths. There's even a Jacuzzi, for total relaxation. By special request and accommodation, guests are permitted to bring children and certain pets. When making your plans, keep in mind that the inn is closed in January. $$; ☐. (662) 665-0044.

SPECIAL EVENTS

Jacinto Fourth of July Festival. Saturday nearest July 4. The Jacinto Courthouse is the site of the Jacinto Fourth of July Festival, with entertainment, Confederate encampments, Chucalissa Indian dance performances, and arts and crafts. The celebration is free and open to the public. (662) 286-8662.

Slugburger Festival. July. Basically, the Slugburger Festival is just an excuse to party in Corinth. Technically, it's a three-day tribute (usually the second weekend in July) to the slugburger (see Borroum's in Where to Eat) and includes entertainment, arts and crafts, food, and rides. (662) 287-1550; (800) 748-9048.

Hog Wild in Corinth Barbecue Festival. September–October. This barbecue contest and festival is a spin-off from famed Memphis in May. There's live music, rides, and, of course, lots of barbecue. (662) 287-5269; (800) 748-9048.

SHILOH

Shiloh isn't but a 20-mile drive north of Corinth. Head north on MS 45. Take a slight right onto MS 2, which becomes TN 22. You'll be in Shiloh in about twenty-five minutes, and you'll still be in the thick of all things Confederate—for it was here on April 6–7, 1862, that one of the bloodiest, most bitter battles of the Civil War was fought by 100,000 soldiers. And it was the battle of Shiloh in particular that precipitated General Grant's important victory at Vicksburg.

WHERE TO GO

Shiloh National Military Park. 1055 Pittsburg Landing, Shiloh, TN 38376. The Shiloh National Military Park was established in 1894, just thirty-two years after the battle. In addition to the battle site itself, which gets the most visitors in April—the month of the actual battle—the park has a visitor center with museum and exhibits and offers guided tours. About every thirty minutes the center runs a film that explains the history of the park and battle. You can also go on a self-guided tour (either on foot or by bicycle) on the many interpretive military and environmental trails throughout the park. Pack a lunch—there are several picnic areas. Overlooking the river are well-preserved prehistoric Indian mounds. Before you leave, check out the park's bookstore for a great selection of military books. The shop is just across the parking lot from the visitor center. Fee. Park (731) 689-5275; bookstore (731) 689-3475.

WHERE TO SHOP

Shiloh's Civil War Relics. 4730 Highway 22, Shiloh, TN 38376. Rafael and Lori Eledge are committed Civil War buffs and have turned their interest into a shop with an enormous collection of authentic (guaranteed!) Shiloh Civil War artifacts. The shop is closed on Tuesday, but visitors can enjoy learning some of the history of the war by browsing the shop every other day of the week. Here's a brief sampling of some of the history the Eledges have for sale: artillery, books, bullets and firearms, medical items, currency and bonds, swords, prints and documents, leather goods, buckles, and buttons. The small admission fee can be applied toward a purchase. ☐. (731) 689-4114.

WHERE TO EAT

Mr. D's BBQ. Highway 57, Shiloh, TN 38376. Locals will tell you Mr. D's has the best barbecue this side of the Mississippi (River, that is). These days Mr. D, short for Mr. Davis, keeps the joint open only on weekends, so be sure to plan your trip around his schedule if you're in the mood for non-Memphis barbecue. In fact, you may want to call ahead to make sure the pork is "on." $-$$. (731) 689-3736.

    Hagy's Catfish Hotel. 1140 Hagy Lane (off TN 22 south), Shiloh, TN 38376. Hagy's is so close to the Tennessee River that the catfish practically jump out of the water and onto your plate. But fear not, the Hagy family, longtime residents of the area, have managed to direct those catfish right into their delicious fry batter (actually, Hagy's fish are farm raised). Whether it's the catfish or the Hagy family name, locals swear by this place, and out-of-towners have been known to drive two hours just for the grub. Closed Monday. $$; ☐. (731) 689-3327.

SPECIAL EVENTS

Civil War reenactments. Throughout the warmer months and especially in April, the Shiloh area is host to authentic Civil War reenactments. Joe Davis of the Shiloh National Military Park (and son of Mr. D himself) can fill you in on any scheduled events or direct you to who's hosting. (731) 689-5275.

    Anniversary of the Battle of Shiloh. April. The anniversary celebration is held on the weekend closest to April 6. Even if you aren't a Civil War buff, this special event has a lot to offer, including a living-history Confederate encampment with skits and demonstrations about life during the Civil War. You'll see artillery, cavalry, and infantry demonstrations. (731) 689-5696.

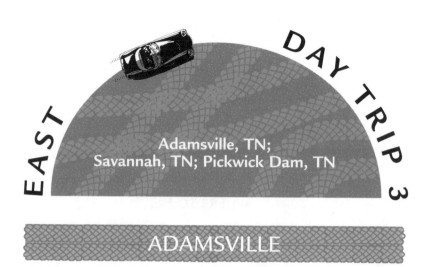

ADAMSVILLE

There are two ways to reach this neck of the Tennessee woods, so you should choose your route based on what other sites you may want to see on your way. The easiest way is through Somerville and Bolivar via US 64 east. Another way is through Corinth and Shiloh: Take US 72 E until you hit TN 22 north, which will hook up with US 64. Before you go the last few miles to Adamsville, though, you may feel like stopping in Crump, Tennessee, where you can check out the weekend flea market. If you decide to breeze on through to the first destination in your day trip, you'll only have 4 more miles. Adamsville is the resting place of Buford Pusser, the infamous sheriff. Stop in at his former home and museum to learn a little local folklore before heading on to Savannah and Pickwick.

WHERE TO GO

Buford Pusser Home and Museum. 342 Pusser Street, Adamsville, TN 38310. Remember the *Walking Tall* ax-wielding sheriff of 1970s movie fame? Well, Buford Pusser, who was shot eight times and knifed seven times, lived and worked in Adamsville. He died in the mid-1970s in a suspicious car accident when his brand-new 1974 Corvette blew up with Pusser behind the wheel. They say it was a "gas explosion," but locals and fans have always questioned this ruling. The charred remains of the car are on display in Pigeon Forge, Tennessee, but the McNairy County sheriff's home and much of his

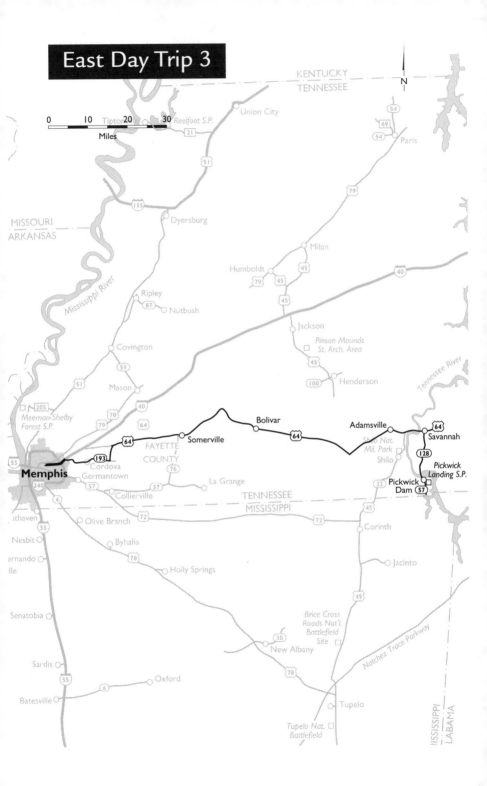

East Day Trip 3

0 10 20 30
Miles

KENTUCKY
TENNESSEE

N

Tipton
Reelfoot S.P.
Union City
54
69
54
Paris
21
51
79
155
Dyersburg
MISSOURI
ARKANSAS
Milan
Humboldt
40
45
79
45
Ripley
87
Nutbush
Jackson
Pinson Mounds
St. Arch. Area
Covington
45
59
100
Henderson
51
Mason
40
70
79
Tennessee River
Meeman-Shelby
Forest S.P.
205
64
64
Somerville
Bolivar
64
Adamsville
64
Savannah
193
FAYETTE
Shilo Nat.
Mil. Park
128
55
Cordova
COUNTY
76
Shilo
Pickwick
Landing S.P.
Memphis
Germantown
57
La Grange
22
Pickwick
57
240
57
Collierville
TENNESSEE
Dam
4
MISSISSIPPI
thaven
55
Olive Branch
72
72
45
Nesbit
Corinth
arnando
78
lle
Byhalia
Holly Springs
Jacinto
Senatobia
45
Brice Cross
Roads Nat'l.
Battlefield
Site
Sardis
30
Natchez Trace Parkway
55
New Albany
6
Oxford
78
Batesville
Tupelo
MISSISSIPPI
ALABAMA
Tupelo Nat.
Battlefield

history remain a popular tourist attraction in Adamsville. There's a Pusser shrine in the museum; his daughter, Dwana, sometimes stops by for a surprise visit. At the gift shop, be sure to pick up a souvenir ax handle. If you're interested, you can visit the graves of both Pusser and his wife, who was killed by an assassin, in the town cemetery. True enthusiasts should time their trip around the Buford Pusser Festival, which is held in May and offers arts and crafts, food and games, and an antique car show. Museum hosts can give you the exact dates of the tribute. Open daily all year. Fee. (901) 632-4080.

SAVANNAH

To get to Savannah, head toward Crump on US 64 and keep going another 4 miles or so, crossing the Tennessee River as you drive. Just on the other side, you'll find Savannah, which was home to Queen Haley, the grandmother of *Roots* author Alex Haley. She died in the 1930s and is buried in the town cemetery. What makes Savannah interesting for Tennesseans is that the Cherokee Indians crossed the Savannah Trail as they made their journey down the Trail of Tears. If you follow along, you'll go through Savannah's historic district and pass important historic landmarks surrounding Alex Haley Sr. as well as the Civil War.

WHERE TO GO

Hardin County Tourism Board. 507 Main Street, Savannah, TN 38372. The tourism office is located inside the Tennessee River Museum and can provide you with brochures and information about the area. Open daily. www.tourhardincnty.org. (731) 925-2364; (800) 552-FUNN.

 Tennessee River Museum. 507 Main Street, Savannah, TN 38372. This museum is a tribute to the Tennessee River, which has been the heart and spirit of the Savannah community since the town was settled in the 1820s. The river has had a strong influence as a transporter of goods and as a part of the beautiful Tennessee land-scape. At the museum, visitors learn about the river through five major exhibits and a collection of American Indian artifacts, Civil

War relics, and other historical finds, including items from paleon-tology digs. Open daily. Fee. (731) 925-2364; (800) 552-FUNN.

Savannah Historic Trail and district. The Savannah Trail was crossed when Cherokee Indians traveled the Trail of Tears. This walking and biking trail takes you through the town's historic district and on to the site where Alex Haley Sr. operated a ferry crossing at the river. From there, the trail moves along the river to Wayne Jerrold's Riverside Park, where the annual Savannah Blue-grass Festival is held every June, and then back to town. Throughout your tour, you can learn about the trail's history via reader boards that line the trail and explain relevant Civil War, Native American mound, and the Trail of Tears information. Within the historic district itself are about twenty buildings (built between 1869 and 1930) of historic importance, especially the Cherry Mansion, which is on the trail route. The Cherry Mansion is supposedly one of the oldest buildings in the town; it's certainly the most famous. During the Civil War, General Ulysses S. Grant converted it into his head-quarters. These days Cherry Mansion is a private residence, but each September the owners welcome the Memphis Symphony Orchestra to their lawn for the Sunset Symphony (bring blankets and a picnic). You can pick up a brochure and get more information at the Tennessee River Museum or the Hardin County Tourism Board. www.tourhardincnty.org. (731) 925-2364; (800) 552-FUNN.

WHERE TO SHOP

Stained Glass Designs. 625 Florence Road, Savannah, TN 38372. Just visiting this shop is fun, but you'll be so mesmerized by the custom-made stained glass that you won't be able to leave without buying something. The Tiffany lamps are especially gorgeous. ☐. (731) 926-2001.

Gift shops. Savannah has several gift shops with everything from candles to tea towels and souvenirs. Don't miss these two along Main Street:

Main Street Gift Gallery. 610 Main Street, Savannah, TN 38372. ☐. (731) 925-3331.

Heritage House Gifts Shop. 410 Main Street West, Savannah, TN 38372 ☐. (731) 925-4907.

WHERE TO EAT AND STAY

White Elephant Bed and Breakfast Inn. 304 Church Street, Savannah, TN 38372. With two stone white elephants flanking its front walk, this B&B is hard to miss. It's in Savannah's historic district, within walking distance of downtown and the river, and can also be found on the National Register of Historic Places. The building itself dates to 1901 and is classic Queen Anne in style, with a circular tower, wraparound front porch, and curved-glass bay windows. Inside the White Elephant are two antiques-furnished parlor rooms with an ample supply of games, books, and Civil War memorabilia. Your hosts, Sharon and Ken Hansgen, will encourage any of the musically inclined to give the fully restored pump organ a try. In the morning you'll enjoy a lavish breakfast in the formal dining room. And if you plan to head out for some Civil War touring, be sure to consult Sharon and Ken, who are Civil War buffs and quite knowledgeable about the nearby battle sites and attractions. Romance and Civil War packages are available. $$; ☐. (731) 925–6410.

   Bellis Botel. TN 128 and Botel Road, Savannah, TN 38372. Most visitors to Bellis Botel don't stay overnight, though four rustic cabins are available to rent; they go to eat and to experience the quirkiness of this remodeled quarterboat riverside resort. *Botel* is short for "boat-hotel." The recreation area, which includes a playground, offers fishing, boat docking and launching, and RV camping with hookups. The restaurant serves breakfast, lunch, and dinner every day except Monday. The Botel's specialty is catfish, and the cook will even prepare your own catch for you and your dining companions. If you've enjoyed enough catfish already, try steak, country-fried chicken, or a sandwich. $–$$; ☐. (731) 925–4787.

WHERE TO EAT

Woody's Restaurant. 705 Main Street, Savannah, TN 38372. Because it's right in the thick of things, Woody's makes for an easy and convenient lunch stop. And true to its proximity to the Tennessee River, this joint serves catfish, along with other tasty southern-style dishes. If you've indulged too many times in catfish during your trips in this area, try a Woody's sandwich or steak. And definitely get a slice of the cheesecake for dessert. Open Monday through Saturday for lunch and dinner; Sunday for lunch. $–$$; □. (731) 925-0104.

PICKWICK DAM

From Savannah, drive southwest on TN 226 to get to TN 128 south (left) and finally TN 57 south (left). It'll take you a total of about twenty minutes to get to the town of Pickwick Dam. Many Memphians head straight for Pickwick because there are so many activities at this destination that it's worth its own trip. So from Memphis, head east on I-40 for about 15 miles and exit onto US 64, which you'll stay on for another 70 or so miles. Take US 45 south about 6 miles and make a left onto TN 57. After about fifteen minutes, you'll be in Pickwick, the town host to the state park, which is located just about on the border of Mississippi and Alabama. During the warm months Memphians flock to the park for summer "fun in the sun," and in fall visitors can catch a beautiful vision of the autumn foliage reflected in the glassy lake water. With so much to do, you'll never run out of reasons to make the two-hour drive again and again every year.

WHERE TO GO

Pickwick Landing State Resort Park. Park Road, Pickwick Dam, TN 38365. In the late 1800s Pickwick Landing served as a riverboat stop, but the Tennessee Valley Authority built a dam here in the 1930s. Forty years later the Tennessee state park system acquired and developed the land, providing an extensive and varied recreation area. With the inn, cabins, marina, and picnic facilities, Pickwick Landing is one of the most popular parks in Tennessee. Today visitors can boat, fish, golf, swim, ski, and camp. www.state.tn.us/environment/parks/pickwick/. (731) 689-3129.

Boating. All types of boats are permitted on the lake, which is accessible by three free-of-charge boat ramps. Gas pumps, transient storage, ice (for coolers), and fishing boat rentals are available at the service center of the Pickwick Marina. (731) 689-5175.

Fishing. Pickwick caters to amateur anglers out for a weekend of relaxation and a few catfish to fry as well as to the true devotee, looking for the biggest bass in the lake. A park ranger at the marina can fill you in on what fish—bass, bream, crappie, catfish, sauger—are biting on the day of your visit.

Hiking. Beginning at the Resort Inn, you can hike 2.5 miles around the lake on an easygoing trail. It's a leisurely walk that people of all ages can enjoy.

Picnicking. Picnic tables are scattered around the lake, and four picnic shelters are either lakeside or have lake views; a fifth is adjacent to a playground. All of the shelters have grills, and two have running water. If you have a large group, you can reserve a pavilion up to a year in advance.

Swimming. Pool swimming is available to inn and cabin guests at the Resort Inn's two swimming facilities. Lake swimming is, of course, open to all. There are three public beaches around the lake, constituting nearly 2 miles of beach swimming: Circle Beach, Sandy Beach, and Bruton Beach. Keep in mind that swimming is not supervised by park officials. All three sites offer public rest rooms.

Camping. Pickwick Resort has forty-eight campsites equipped with hookups (call for specifics), picnic tables, and grills. At the north-shore Bruton Branch Recreation Area, which is a primitive campground, there are one hundred tent sites, a bathhouse, picnic area, playground, and boat ramp. The tent sites are first come, first served, so set up early. You can reach Bruton Branch via TN 128. (731) 689-3135, ext. 337.

Pickwick Landing State Park Golf Course. Awarded three stars by *Golf Digest,* the Pickwick golf course is a popular and challenging excursion for visitors to the state park. Each hole is lined by trees, and eight have water. Twenty-one bunkers are scattered throughout the course. Packages, including lodging and meals, are available. The course is open every day of the year, except Christmas, and requires tee times (call ahead). (731) 689-3149; (800) 250-8615.

Pickwick Landing Dam. TN 128, Pickwick Dam, TN 38365. The dam is the reason behind Pickwick Landing State Resort Park. Back in 1934 the Tennessee Valley Authority built the dam; within four years the 53-mile-long lake was filling with water. The dam itself is 113 feet high and more than 7,000 feet long. It generates hydroelectric power and provides flood control to the area, along with a waterway for barges and towboats. Children especially enjoy watching the boats lock through the dam, and adults can tour the museum. Free. (731) 925-4346.

WHERE TO EAT AND STAY

Pickwick Landing State Resort Inn. If camping and cabins are a bit too rustic for you, check out the Pickwick Resort Inn, with picturesque views of the lake. In addition to the seventy-five rooms and three suites, there are tennis courts, adult and child swimming pools, and a playground. A wood-paneled dining room serves a variety of meals, both buffet-style and a la carte, at affordable prices. If you're going to Pickwick with a large group, call ahead and the restaurant will cater your lunch or dinner with everything from barbecue to lobster! $$; □. (731) 689-3135; (800) 250-8615.

Cabins at Pickwick Landing State Resort. The cabins are located just next door to the inn and offer guests all the recreational privileges inn guests enjoy. Each cabin has its own fireplace, patio, TV, four double beds, central heat and air, linens, cookware, and a small but very functional kitchen. Guests can book cabins up to one year in advance. $$-$$$. (731) 689-3135; (800) 250-8615.

SOMERVILLE

Take Poplar Avenue east; it will turn into US 72. Stay straight on US 72. Turn left onto MS 57. Make another left, onto TN 76. When you arrive in Somerville, Tennessee, you will be amazed at the outstanding plantation homes and captivated by the delightful town square. If you spend your free time participating in field activities, you won't want to miss the exhibits at the Bird Dog Museum. For those who enjoy viewing and touring pre–Civil War buildings, the Architectural Treasures of Fayette County Tour is sure to please—each year a number of buildings and residences are open to the public for touring.

WHERE TO GO

Fayette County Chamber of Commerce. 107 West Court Square, Somerville, TN 38068. Because there are so many fabulous antebellum homes in this area, you'll want to stop by the chamber of commerce to get directions and information about which ones are open for touring at various times throughout the year. (901) 465-8690.

Ames Plantation. Ames Drive, Grand Junction, TN 38039. Ames Plantation is home of the National Field Trial Championship, and one of eleven branch agricultural experiment stations for the University of Tennessee. The land itself is privately owned and oper-

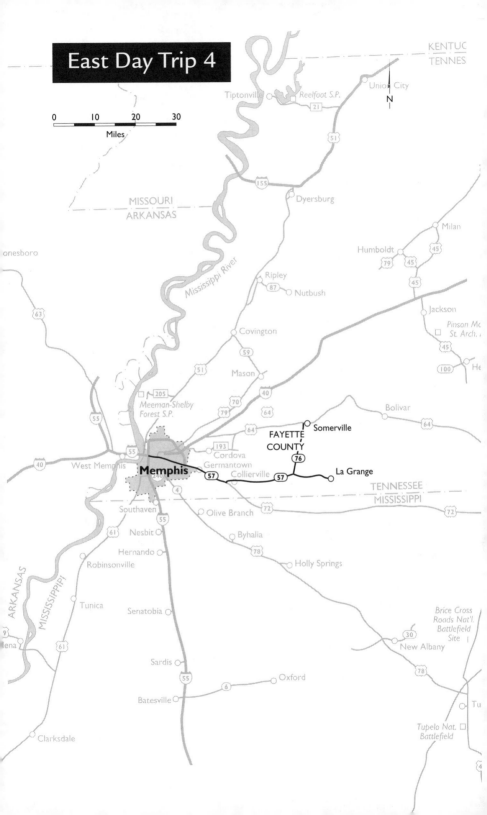

East Day Trip 4

0   10   20   30
Miles

KENTUC
TENNES

N

Tiptonville   Reelfoot S.P.   Union City
21

51

155

Dyersburg

MISSOURI
ARKANSAS

Milan

Humboldt   45
79   45

onesboro

45

Ripley   Nutbush
87   Jackson

63   Pinson Mc
St. Arch.

Covington   45

59   100   He

Mason
51

205   70   40
Meeman-Shelby   79   64   Bolivar
Forest S.P.   64

55   64   Somerville   64
FAYETTE
193   COUNTY
West Memphis   Cordova   76
40   55   Germantown   La Grange
Memphis   57   Collierville   57
Mississippi River   TENNESSEE
4   MISSISSIPPI

Southaven   72
55

Nesbit   Olive Branch

78
Hernando   Byhalia
Robinsonville   Holly Springs

ARKANSAS   Brice Cross
MISSISSIPPI   Roads Nat'l.
Senatobia   Battlefield
9   30   Site
ena   61   New Albany

Sardis   78
55

Batesville   6   Oxford   Tu

Clarksdale   Tupelo Nat.
Battlefield   4

ated by the trustees of the Hobart Ames Foundation as was instructed in the will of the late Julia C. Ames. Ames donated the 18,567 acres for research and educational purposes. Visitors to the Ames Plantation can stroll the grounds and tour the nineteenth-century farmstead. Along the way, stop in the cemetery to see where more than twenty memorials mark the burial of West Tennessee residents. Throughout the year, staff at the Ames Plantation offer a number of camps and classes for the outdoor enthusiast. (901) 878-1067.

The Bird Dog Museum. 505 Highway 57 West, Grand Junction, TN 38039. This museum pays tribute to more than one hundred years of sporting tradition. You'll find a storehouse of information, art, sculpture, photography, and memorabilia dedicated to field activities with man's best friend. Among the artwork and exhibits contained in the museum, discover some of history's most famous bird dogs. Not to be surpassed by other famous museums, the Bird Dog Museum has its own version of the Mona Lisa—a re-creation depicting a bird dog instead of a woman. The eyes seem to follow you at every angle. Closed Monday. Admission fee. (901) 764-2058.

WHERE TO SHOP

The Magic Forest. 111 West Court Square, Somerville, TN 38068. Nestled along the town square, the Magic Forest is a truly whimsical store. Items for sale include antiques, glassware and knickknacks, quilts, artificial and silk floral arrangements, and jewelry. The store also features a wide variety of gift items and collectibles, including a large selection of designer Barbie dolls. Open weekdays. (901) 465-0077.

Court Square. Somerville, TN. Along this delightful small-town square, you'll find myriad art shops, antiques stores, the courthouse, the chamber of commerce, and restaurants. As part of a revitalization project, the square has been spruced up with new walkways and old-time street lamps.

WHERE TO EAT

Silver Moon Cafeteria. West Court Square, Somerville, TN 38068. Owner Eula May Richardson has turned the Silver Moon Cafeteria into much more than just an eatery here in Somerville. While she serves a variety of hot meals cafeteria-style almost daily, it's the "round table" that has made its mark in town. The locals gather at Silver Moon to discuss politics and goings-on around town here at the table. If you want to catch up on the town gossip, this is the place to be. You won't be disappointed by the food, either. Closed Thursday and Sunday. $-$$. (901) 465-2728.

Me and My Tea Room. 111 West Court Square, Somerville, TN 38068. This tearoom, which is located in the Magic Forest gift shop, features a fresh-brewed tea of the day. Like the tea selection, the lunch menu changes daily, but you can be sure the delectable fare will include both home-style and gourmet creations compliments of owner Catherine Bowling. Home-baked breads and desserts can be enjoyed in the tearoom or taken home, and Bowling also sells tasty casseroles to go. Another specialty: made-from-scratch wedding cakes. While Me and My Tea Room isn't open to the general public for dinner, Bowling will whip together a memorable dinner for parties of eight or more. Closed Monday. $-$$; ☐. (901) 465-0077.

The Hut. 16920 Highway 64, Somerville, TN 38068. If you're looking for some great southern cuisine, look no farther. While the Hut features a variety of plate lunches ranging from barbecue to catfish, it's the desserts you'll want to save room for. With a selection of homemade pies ranging from chocolate to coconut, lemon icebox, pecan, and German chocolate, you'll have a tough time deciding which one to try. Open daily. $-$$. (901) 465-3458.

SPECIAL EVENTS

Architectural Treasures of Fayette County Tour. Annually, more than twenty-five homeowners open their doors during the Architectural Treasures of Fayette County Tour. One of the more popular spots is Frogmore, the oldest of the pre–Civil War buildings located in Somerville. Frogmore was built circa 1829 and has remained in the same family since then. These homes, many of which are listed on the National Register of Historic Places, represent a number of period styles dating from as early as the 1800s and vary from year to year. For information about this tour, call the Fayette County Chamber of Commerce. (901) 465-8690.

LA GRANGE

La Grange is the oldest town in Fayette County. It began as a Chickasaw Indian village named Itey Uch La, which means "cluster of pines." La Grange originally served as a trading post for the Indians, who frequently visited the town. Located on a bluff overlooking northern Mississippi and just 50 miles from Memphis, this destination is a historic treat for anyone who enjoys touring antebellum homes and old plantations. Some of the stops include the Parsonage, Hancock Hall, and Westover of Woodstock. From Somerville, return to TN 57 via TN 76 and turn east toward La Grange.

WHERE TO GO

The historic district. Fayette County Chamber of Commerce, 107 West Court Square, Somerville, TN 38068. La Grange boasts a number of distinguished homes along the streets of its historic district. While many of them are currently private residences, others are open for touring at various times throughout the year. For more information and for addresses for all historic homes, contact the chamber of commerce. Below are some of the homes featured in La Grange's historic district. (901) 465-8690.

Hancock Hall. This home, which was completed in 1857, was built by Dr. J. J. Pulliam. According to historical records, Yankee officers took possession of the house in 1861, leaving only a tiny portion of the home for the Pulliam family, and remained in the house until after the end of the Civil War. Union general Hurlbut's headquarters was located on the front lawn of the home, while soldiers pitched their tents in the field in behind it. Today it's a private residence.

Woodlawn Plantation. This noble Greek Revival home was built in 1828 by Major Charles Michie, a veteran of the War of 1812, who financed it through a land grant given for his military services. In 1862 Woodlawn became the West Tennessee headquarters for General William T. Sherman and was used as an emergency hospital during the war. It's rumored that Ulysses S. Grant visited Woodlawn during the war. In 1875 Dr. J. J. Pulliam, who also built Hancock Hall, bought Woodlawn and used it as an office for his medical practice. Today Woodlawn Plantation contains many of the original furnishings and, although it's a private residence, can be viewed by the public on various home tours.

Westover of Woodstock. Records indicate this house was purchased in 1829 by Colonel Philemon Holcombe, a Revolutionary War hero. Westover of Woodstock was the home of Lucy Holcombe, born in 1832 in La Grange. She was the only woman featured on money minted by the Confederacy, which earned her the nickname Queen of the Confederacy because she sold her own rare jewels from Russia to outfit a Confederate army unit. The house was eventually sold to La Grange Female College, where it was used as a dormitory.

The Parsonage. Built in the style that was common during the antebellum period, the Parsonage is referred to as "plantation plain." The home was originally built by a La Grange citizen who fell into debt. At the turn of the twentieth century, the Parsonage earned its name when it became the property of the Methodist Episcopal Church South, which used it as a parsonage for the circuit-rider preacher who frequented the churches in La Grange, Moscow, and Rossville. The house was used as a parsonage until 1940, when it was sold as a private residence.

WHERE TO SHOP

La Grange General Store. 20 Main Street, La Grange, TN 38046. The La Grange General Store began in the early 1890s as Pankey's Store. The store provides a stroll down memory lane to a time when cotton was king and rural life dependent upon the town's merchants. Because the store doesn't operate on a regular schedule, please call the proprietors of the La Grange Inn to make plans for visiting. (901) 878-1000.

WHERE TO STAY

La Grange Inn. 240 Pine Street, La Grange, TN 38046. It's only fitting that such a charming town should feature this enchanting spot to sojourn. The La Grange Inn is made up of three restored railroad overnight houses, which were moved to La Grange from their original spot in Whiteville, Tennessee. The inn itself is located along what's now the Norfolk & Southern Railroad.

The houses of the La Grange Inn provide five private cottage-style accommodations, each with a bedroom, bathroom, and sitting room. The inn also boasts wood-burning fireplaces, private entrances, and porches. Besides the tranquil setting, a health spa is also available, and visitors are greeted with a rousing continental breakfast. During your stay, take part in a canoe trip down the Wolf River or spend the day biking or hiking the rural area. Because the inn is open seasonally, make reservations well in advance with proprietors Nora and Wallace Witmer. (901) 878–1000.

BYHALIA

It seems fitting that a place as simple and down to earth as Byhalia, Mississippi, can be visited with an easy one-step trip. Take US 78 south. You'll run smack dab into downtown, where the local chamber of commerce has been steadily renovating and revitalizing the town's turn-of-the-twentieth-century buildings for the last couple of years. Nearly all of Byhalia's residents boast of its small-town feeling and many are second- or third-generation locals. Byhalia is the kind of place you're born and raised in, not the kind of place you move to. But it is a charming spot to visit. Part of the town was even added to the National Register of Historic Places. When you arrive, just park your car and stroll along Church Street, Byhalia's main drag. Here you'll find everything you need: places to shop, eat, and even stay.

WHERE TO SHOP

Magnolia Manor Antiques. 2457 Church Street, Byhalia, MS 38611. Magnolia Manor is just across the street from the Southern Corner Café and makes a nice after-lunch stop to let your hearty meal settle in. Shoppers enjoy browsing the knickknacks, antique furnishings, and dishware. One interesting line that Magnolia Manor carries is antique hardware. If you look hard enough, you may find a great deal on some nineteenth-century hinges or a Victorian hutch. (662) 838–9820.

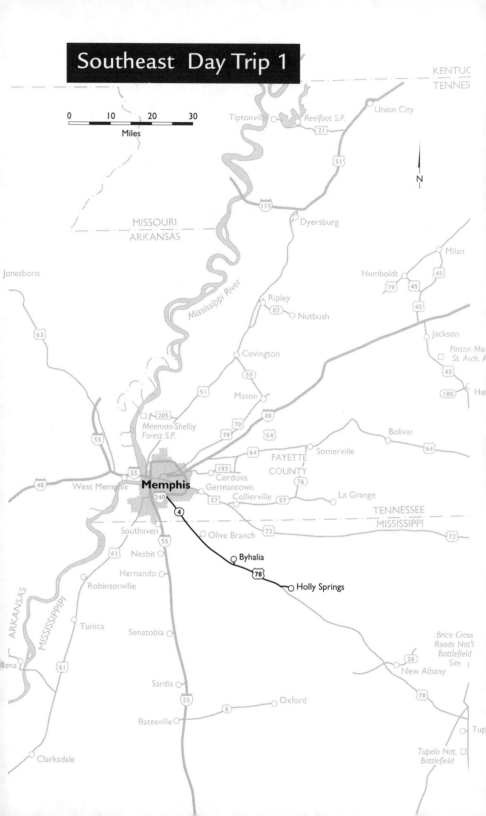

0   10   20   30
Miles

KENTUCKY
TENNESSEE

Tiptonville
Reelfoot S.P.
Union City
21

51
155

Dyersburg

MISSOURI
ARKANSAS

Milan

Jonesboro

Humboldt
79   45   45

63
Ripley
87   Nutbush
45

Jackson

Pinson Mo
St. Arch. A
45

Mississippi River

Covington
59
100   He

Mason
51
40
64

Meeman-Shelby
Forest S.P.
205
70
79
64
Bolivar

55
193   64
FAYETTE
Somerville
64

Memphis
240
Cordova
Germantown
COUNTY
76
La Grange

West Memphis
55
57   Collierville   57
TENNESSEE
MISSISSIPPI

40
4
Southaven
55
Olive Branch
72
72

61
Nesbit
Byhalia
78

Hernando
Holly Springs

Robinsonville
ARKANSAS
MISSISSIPPI

Tunica
Senatobia
Brice Cross
Roads Nat'l.
Battlefield
Site
30
New Albany

lena
61

Sardis
55
Oxford
78

Batesville
6

Clarksdale
Tupelo Nat.
Battlefield

N

WHERE TO EAT

Southern Corner Café. 2443 Church Street, Byhalia, MS 38611. Located just as its name suggests—on the southern corner of Byhalia's main intersection, the Southern Corner Café gets a lot of local business. Everyone in here knows everyone else by name, even *nickname.* But visitors aren't left out of the camaraderie: Just sit down and dive into the sweet southern charm. Menu offerings include the standard cafe/diner fare of sandwiches, soup and salad, and plates of meat and vegetables. $-$$; □. (662) 838-2068.

WHERE TO STAY

The Carriage House Bed and Breakfast. 2460 Church Street, Byhalia, MS 38611. Your hosts at the Carriage House B&B, Scooter and Sonia Dempsey, are longtime Byhalia residents and devotees. In the early 1990s the Dempseys bought and began renovating their 1906 home that had a carriage house out back. This carriage house is now the B&B. It's basically just a one-bedroom gig, but up to four people can sleep here. And it's the only place in town to spend the night. The bedroom has a chandelier and antique bed with canopy, making it a romantic and intimate setting for couples. After a traditional southern or continental breakfast, guests tour the garden, complete with ducks, a pond, and fountain. As a guest, you'll have access to the property's pool, and you'll definitely want to wander into Sonia's floral shop, called the Blossom Shop, where you can take a minute to smell the roses. $$; □. (662) 838-3535; (662) 838-4402.

SPECIAL EVENTS

White Oak Fall Festival. October. White Oak is the definition of *small-town festival* with its arts and crafts, concession food, and local entertainment. (662) 838-2132.

HOLLY SPRINGS

Just jump back onto US 78 south for about ten or fifteen minutes, and you'll find yourself in Holly Springs, the seat of Marshall

County, Mississippi. Although Memphians go to Holly Springs for its natural and historical points of interest—including Holly Springs National Forest and the Marshall County Historical Museum, with an interesting Civil War collection—many also go to hunt quail. This is traditional quail country and about one hundred years ago inspired the National Field Trials.

WHERE TO GO

Holly Springs Chamber of Commerce. 154 South Memphis Street, Holly Springs, MS 38635. The chamber can provide visitors with maps and information about the area. Open weekdays. (662) 252-2943.

Holly Springs National Forest. Lake Center exit off TN 78 east. Seven miles east of Holly Springs and covering more than 150,000 acres across north-central Mississippi, Holly Springs National Forest nearly reaches Tennessee. Visitors enjoy fishing in the lakes, camping, and picnicking, but hiking is the most popular activity at the park. If you're up for a challenge, try the 4.5-mile Chewalla Lake Hiking Trail. Not for leisurely strolls, this trail is difficult because of both its length and its primitive pathway. From the Chewalla recreation center, you'll tour the lake going south and looping around the northeast to finish at Johnston Mill Pond. If you want a less physically taxing but more educational hike, walk along the Pushkas Lake Hiking Trail, which has interpretive signs guiding you along an environmental learning path. Contact the park office in Oxford, Mississippi, for more information. (662) 236-6550.

Marshall County Historical Museum. 220 East College Avenue, Holly Springs, MS 38635. This museum houses a wonderful collection of Civil War artifacts. Because Holly Springs was the site of sixty-two Union raids, there remains an interesting and varied range of memorabilia dating to the late 1800s. Particular to this museum is the array of military garb. Other artifacts include tools and machinery, women's clothing, and antique furnishings. The museum is open every day but Sunday and major holidays. (601) 252-3669.

Dunn's Shooting Grounds. 532 Quailwood Road, Holly Springs, MS 38635. Any hunter will tell you that northern Mississippi is quail country, and a good hunter will direct you to Dunn's, the 900-acre shooting ground less than an hour from Memphis. Here you'll find expert guides and trained dogs to help with wing-shooting and plantation quail hunting. Dunn's also operates a full-stocked clay-bird range within a 1,000-square-foot shooting pavilion. Your hunt fee for a half or full day includes a bird count; dressing and packaging; field transportation; and guides and dogs. After a day of quail hunting or trapshooting, you can enjoy both a dinner of southern cuisine and a peaceful night's sleep at the nearly 4,000-square-foot lodge. There are eight air-conditioned guest rooms with private bath. (662) 564-1111; (800) 564-1111.

WHERE TO STAY

Fort Daniel Hall Bed and Breakfast. 184 South Memphis Road, Holly Springs, MS 38635. Imagine George Washington's house, Mount Vernon: American Colonial with strong box columns and a lazy-afternoon veranda. Fort Daniel Hall Bed and Breakfast, known in the history books as Fort Daniel Place, is Mississippi's own classic 1850s southern antebellum home. Through the years the owners have tried to maintain Fort Daniel's original structure and crafts-manship while renovating the interior to provide a truly warm and gracious stay for guests. There are three air-conditioned bedrooms with a variety of sleeping arrangements. For ultimate privacy, guests can stay in the coach house, also on the property. Antique furniture and objets d'arts, adorn the interior of the B&B; the smaller pieces are available for purchase. Breakfast is included in your room rate, and for an extra charge the cook will whip up a southern-style lunch or dinner for four or more guests. $$; ☐. (662) 252-4447.

Heritage Inn. US 78 at Highways 7 and 4, Holly Springs, MS 38635. The Heritage Inn is a basic travel-lodge hotel for families. There are forty-eight rooms, along with a pool and restaurant on site. Ask about package deals, which include golfing at the nearby Kirkwood National Golf Course, and a seniors' discount. $$; ☐. (662) 252-1120.

SPECIAL EVENTS

Holly Springs Pilgrimage. April. East 125 South Maury, Holly Springs, MS 38635. Although it only happens once a year, the Holly Springs Pilgrimage is comprehensive in its historical significance and value. Costumed hosts from the Holly Springs Garden Club will take you on a history tour of the Hill Crest Cemetery. You'll also tour homes and churches featured on the National Register of Historic Places. The garden clubbers always make sure to get a few particularly lovely gardens in the tour route. (662) 252-7307.

Kudzu Festival. July. Yet another barbecue contest (and you thought kudzu was just an annoying plant!). Held every year in the middle of summer, the Kudzu Festival is a favorite among locals, with music, talent shows, arts and crafts, food, and even a carnival. (662) 252-2943.

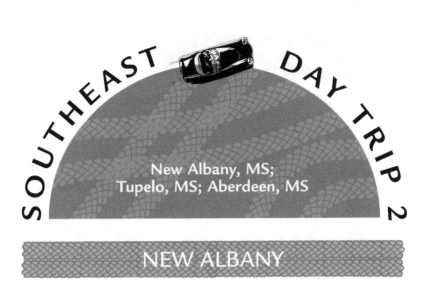

SOUTHEAST DAY TRIP 2

New Albany, MS;
Tupelo, MS; Aberdeen, MS

NEW ALBANY

With Nonconnah Parkway reaching all the way to US 78, it's almost all four-lane roads and 65-miles-per-hour speed limits to New Albany, making this drive a cinch. There's not much to see in northern Mississippi; a Texaco just outside Byhalia is about the only shopping for the hour and a half you're on the road. But once you reach your destination, you'll be able to do a lot of shopping at one of the area's two major flea markets (the other is in Tupelo). New Albany itself is right on the edge of the highway, where it intersects with MS 15 and MS 30. If you're keeping your eye on the turnoffs, you can't miss it.

WHERE TO GO

New Albany Flea Market. 514 West Bankhead, New Albany, MS 38652. Open Monday through Saturday from 9:00 A.M. to 6:00 P.M., the New Albany Flea Market is a sure thing. Around 200 people each day come to browse the booths, which sell a variety of merchandise, such as antiques, candles, jewelry, heritage lace, and pottery. (662) 534-0370.

WHERE TO STAY

Heritage House. 307 East Main Street, New Albany, MS 38652. Built nearly one hundred years ago in New Albany, this historic home has sweeping front steps and a splendid front porch. It also

77

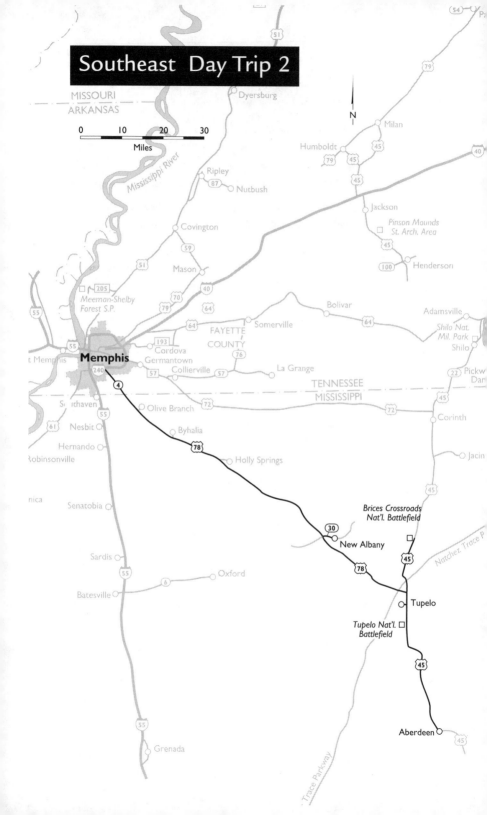

Southeast Day Trip 2

MISSOURI
ARKANSAS

Dyersburg

Miles
0   10   20   30

Mississippi River

N

Milan

Ripley
Nutbush

Humboldt

Covington

Jackson

Pinson Mounds
St. Arch. Area

Mason

Henderson

Meeman-Shelby
Forest S.P.

Bolivar

Adamsville

Shilo Nat.
Mil. Park

Shilo

Memphis

FAYETTE
COUNTY

Somerville

Cordova
Germantown
Collierville

La Grange

Pickw
Dar

TENNESSEE
MISSISSIPPI

t Memphis

Corinth

Southaven

Olive Branch

Nesbit

Byhalia

Jacin

Hernando

Holly Springs

Robinsonville

Brices Crossroads
Nat'l. Battlefield

Senatobia

New Albany

Natchez Trace P

Sardis

Oxford

Tupelo

Batesville

Tupelo Nat'l.
Battlefield

Grenada

Aberdeen

Trace Parkway

offers guests a choice of six bedrooms, including a two-bedroom suite with sitting room and television. Visitors to Heritage House enjoy the quiet surrounding neighborhood in addition to the antique furnishings and 12-foot ceilings. Most relax in the shade of that great front porch after breakfast each morning to peruse the newspaper. One particularly nice aspect of this inn is that it welcomes children. If you're traveling along the Natchez Trace, Heritage House is an easy twenty-minute drive away. Rates are slightly higher on weekends. $$; ☐. (662) 538-1048.

Holiday Inn Express Hotel and Suites. 300 Highway 30 West, New Albany, MS 38652. If you're more comfortable at a familiar nationwide hotel, try the Holiday Inn, where you'll get continental breakfast and free local calls to scout the area before heading out to explore for the day. The suites are especially nice for families, with kitchenettes and more room to spread out. This hotel is also handi-capped accessible. The suites are often only $30 more than a stan-dard room. $$; ☐. (662) 534-8870.

SPECIAL EVENTS

Union County Fair and Livestock Show. August. This is an old-fashioned, rural county fair complete with rodeo and carnival. (662) 534-1916.

TUPELO

Tupelo is just another fifteen minutes or so beyond New Albany. Get back onto US 78 south (actually, southeast) and take the exit for US 45 south. You'll be in Tupelo—the birthplace of Elvis Presley and the site of the battle of Tupelo—in no time. Because it has "modern" as well as "old" history, Tupelo is an appealing destination. There are several Elvis attractions, all within the scope of the Elvis Presley Center and Museum. In addition, you can visit the historic battle of Tupelo site, where in July 1864 Confederate soldiers met Union soldiers in one of the Civil War's fiercest contests. Tupelo is also home to the Gigantic Flea Market—and it really is gigantic. People from miles around make the drive to pick up knickknacks at the market and home furnishings at the very well-known Flowerdale emporium.

WHERE TO GO

Tupelo Convention and Visitors Bureau. 399 East Main Street, Tupelo, MS 38804. The tourist office can provide visitors with maps and information about the area. Open weekdays. (662) 841-6521; (800) 533-0611.

Oren Dunn City Museum of Tupelo. Highway 6 West at James L. Ballard Park, Tupelo, MS 38804. Tupelo's city museum has an impressive collection of 2,000 artifacts, all evidence of northeast Mississippi's rich and diverse history, which includes Elvis and Chickasaw Indians. The exhibits are displayed in a former dairy barn, where Jersey cows were once raised. The main attractions are the space exhibit, with several flags carried to and from the moon, dinosaur fossils, and a re-created Chickasaw hut and nineteenth-century village. Fee. Open every day except holidays. (662) 841-6438.

Brices Crossroads National Battlefield. 607 Grisham Road, Baldwyn, MS 38824. Not far from Tupelo up US 45 and onto MS 370 is the famous Brices Crossroads National Battlefield. Brices Crossroads is the spot where, on June 10, 1864, Confederate soldiers beat Union troops. The victory was a major one for General Nathan Bedford Forrest because it forced the Union army back to Memphis. Ultimately, however, the battle proved futile, as it never succeeded in thwarting General William Sherman's productive shipment of supplies to Union troops throughout Tennessee and northeast Mississippi. A one-acre site maintained by the National Park Service features a monument, two cannons, and educational signs depicting the area and event. The Brices Crossroads Visitors and Interpretive Center offers an exhibit featuring Civil War artifacts, a battlefield diorama, and interactive exhibits. An additional 836 acres surrounding the site have been purchased for preservation; big plans are in the works for developing this land. Open Tuesday through Sunday. Fee. (662) 365-3969.

Tupelo National Battlefield. West Main at Monument Street (downtown), Tupelo, MS 38804. Though defeated, the Union soldiers didn't stop at Brices Crossroads. By July 1864 they were headed to Tupelo, where once again Confederate soldiers met them with one of the bloodiest battles of the Civil War. Still leading his men against the campaign of Union general Sherman, Confederate general Forrest had brought his men here to Tupelo in the hope of finally impeding Sherman's supply line for the Union army. History books tell us that Sherman was so determined to win the battle of Tupelo that he told Union leaders to "make up a force and go out to follow Forrest to the death, if it costs 10,000 lives and breaks the Treasury." Despite a grueling effort on the part of the Confederacy, Sherman's campaign continued to manage an effective rail line to supply its Union soldiers. As at Brices Crossroads, the National Park Service operates the Tupelo National Battlefield and provides educational signs explaining the battle and maps depicting the site. The historical site is actually at the center of Tupelo, at the corner of West Main and Monument Streets, where it occupies a park. Free. (662) 680–4025; (800) 305–7417.

Private John Allen National Fish Hatchery. 111 Elizabeth Street, Tupelo, MS 38804. Granted, a fish hatchery doesn't sound too glamorous, but the National Fish Hatchery in Tupelo is definitely a sight to behold. Even *weddings* are performed here. The real business of the hatchery is, of course, hatching fish (for restocking programs across the country), and it's operated by the US Fish and Wildlife Service. But the fun and frivolous aspects of this attraction are the grounds and turn-of-the-twentieth-century Victorian house, maintained by none other than the Tupelo Garden Club. Hence, the weddings. Horticulturists have taken great care to manicure the grounds of the hatchery with plants fitting the style of the 1903 home. There's even a wildlife area for observation and guides who can take you on a tour of the grounds. Guests often bring a gourmet picnic lunch. (662) 842–1341.

Elvis Presley Center and Museum. 306 Elvis Presley Drive, Tupelo, MS 38804. If you're a Memphian, you know why we go to Tupelo: Elvis. Before Graceland, Elvis Presley called Tupelo home. Fans young and old should stop by the Elvis Presley Center and Museum, which displays a wonderfully varied collection of Elvis memorabilia. The word most often used to describe the collection is *unique*. While Graceland focuses on Elvis's musical career (gold records, costumes), the museum in Tupelo takes you all the way back to his childhood, with personal mementos of the Presleys, and then brings you up to the time of his Las Vegas act. The theme is "Times and Things Remembered," and most people around the museum don't even call Elvis by name; he's The King. The museum is part of the larger conglomeration of the Elvis Presley Center, which also includes the birthplace, the Memorial Chapel, and the Elvis Presley Park, with complete recreational facilities for picnics and community events. In addition, the center provides a driving tour map outlining all of the Tupelo landmarks significant to Elvis's early life, such as his grade school, his church, and the hardware store where Elvis bought his first guitar. The center and museum are open seven days a week, except Thanksgiving and Christmas. (662) 841–1245.

Elvis Presley Birthplace. 306 Elvis Presley Drive, Tupelo, MS 38804. The truly serious Elvis aficionado must make a visit to the two-room house in which The King was born on January 8, 1935. It still stands as the most popular modern-history site in the town. According to town folklore, Vernon Presley, Elvis's father, took the materials on loan and built the house himself for less than $200. Elvis was always proud of where he came from and sometimes returned to the house even after attaining fame and glory as the King of Rock and Roll. The birthplace has been restored to the period when Elvis and his family lived there and is a stop along the Elvis Presley Center's driving tour. It's heartwarming to see how Elvis began, and to realize how far he traveled to get to Graceland. Open seven days a week, except Thanksgiving and Christmas. (662) 841–1245.

WHERE TO SHOP

Flowerdale Marketplace. 2025 McCullough Boulevard, Tupelo, MS 38801. Flowerdale is like a home decorating mall, full of shops offering everything from new furnishings to antiques, art to rugs. In between browsing, sit down at Carmita's Café, carefully tucked away at the back of the marketplace. Carmita's always features tantalizing specials to keep you on your toes. ☐. (662) 840–8842.

Tupelo Gigantic Flea Market. 1301 Coley Road, Tupelo, MS 38801. The Gigantic Flea Market is held the second weekend of each month—except February and August, when the Tupelo Furniture Market is in session and brings 30,000 buyers and exhibitors from all around the country. Because the flea market opens only once every four weeks, people from all the around the region make it a scheduled outing on their monthly calendars. The Gigantic has standard flea market merchandise and concession food, but regulars always grab a fried corn fritter on their way in. (601) 842-4442.

WHERE TO EAT

Vanelli's. 1302 North Gloster Street, Tupelo, MS 38804. Bill Kapenekas, the owner, is quite a hit in Tupelo, and so is Vanelli's. Bill is well known around town for his exuberant personality and tasty Greek-Italian dishes. Vanelli's other claim to fame is the John Lennon art that Kapenekas has collected over the years. In addition to the ethnic specials, Vanelli's offers pizza, a buffet, and a variety of American dishes. All in all, it's a casual dining experience with great food. On weekends when big games are on, it becomes a bit of a sports bar. $$; ☐. (662) 844-4410.

S.O.B.'s—Shrimp and Oyster Bar. 1721 North Gloster Street, Tupelo, MS 38804. S.O.B.'s (yup, that's what it's called) is a locally owned shrimp and oyster bar. In addition to the seafood, diners go for the atmosphere, which is somewhat loud and always entertaining. The menu includes oysters on the half shell, hand-battered appetizers, and prime roast beef. $$; ☐. (662) 840-5106.

Park Heights. 825 West Jefferson Street, Tupelo, MS 38804. Park Heights is the newest upscale restaurant in town. Those who know Blair Bean, the owner, use the word *flair* to describe both the woman herself and her restaurant. Flair Blair offers an interesting array of creative cuisine, including goat cheese and prosciutto salad, beef tenderloin with blue cheese grits, and sea bass with Thai tamarind sauce. $$$; ☐. (662) 842-5665.

Gloster 205. 205 North Gloster Street, Tupelo, MS 38804. Located in an old house, Gloster 205 is a long-standing Tupelo tradition: tried and true. It's high end; it's charming; it's quaint; and it's delicious. The menu is all-American: steaks, seafood, prime rib, and salads. $$$; ☐. (662) 842-7205.

WHERE TO STAY

Mockingbird Inn Bed and Breakfast. 305 North Gloster Street, Tupelo, MS 38801. The Mockingbird Inn is located in downtown Tupelo just across the street from Elvis's former school, but Sharon Robertson, the innkeeper, has made her place famous in its own right by creating a "theme" B&B. Within each of the seven bedrooms—all with private bath and telephone—guests will find treasures from a different place in the world: Venice, Mackinac Island, Paris, Athens, Africa, Sanibel Island, and Bavaria. The house itself, however, exudes southern warmth as only a place in Mississippi can. The gazebo, porch swing, and sunporch, along with the inn's main parlor, all bring you back "home" to the South. As part of your stay, you'll receive both a lavish breakfast and an evening treat. Guests also have access to the main dining room for beverages throughout their stay. If you're looking for something extra special, ask Sharon about the inn's Romance Package, which includes an in-room massage and moonlit carriage ride. The Mockingbird has been featured in the international magazine *Travel & Leisure*. It's slightly more expensive on weekends. $$; ☐. (662) 841-0286.

SPECIAL EVENTS

The Elvis Presley Festival. June. Held on the downtown streets of Tupelo, the Tupelo Elvis Presley Festival is a hometown tribute to the King of Rock and Roll. Indulge in music, food, and fun for the entire family. (662) 841-1245.

Battle of Tupelo reenactment. October. This Civil War reenactment includes a variety of living-history events, such as camp demonstrations, skirmishes, and cavalry. Participation is a key factor in making this event a success. Participants practice for much of the year, and onlookers always enjoy a lively show. (662) 841-6438.

ABERDEEN

If you want to go a little farther on your day trip, continue south on US 45 for about ten minutes. Once you reach Shannon, Mississippi, be sure to stay on US 45 proper (it forks southwest as Alt US 45, heading toward West Point and Tombigbee). Aberdeen, about ten more minutes on US 45, is a true small town with less than 7,000 residents, but it has a great bed-and-breakfast to recommend itself. If you happen to go in April, you'll be able to catch the town's beautiful antebellum homes on the Aberdeen Spring Pilgrimage.

WHERE TO STAY

Huckleberry Inn. 500 South Hickory Street, Aberdeen, MS 39730. The Huckleberry Inn comes complete with a traditional white picket fence: you'll feel like you've stumbled into Mayberry. It was built in 1908 and is on the National Register of Historic Places, along with most of the other buildings in the historic district. The inn is the perfect point from which to start a leisurely stroll around the district, admiring the architecture and history of Aberdeen. The innkeepers, Paula and Wayne Thorpe, can direct you to particularly interesting places nearby. There are eight rooms at the Huckleberry, all with private bath and complimentary sherry. Included in your room rate is breakfast, with the inn's signature dish—blueberry French toast—and afternoon tea, accompanied by dessert and fruit. $$; □. (662) 369-7294; (800) 565-7294.

SPECIAL EVENTS

Aberdeen Spring Pilgrimage. April. Costumed guides will take you on a narrated tour of Aberdeen's antebellum and Victorian homes. Contact the Aberdeen Visitors Bureau for more information about all special events. (662) 369-9440; (800) 634-3538.

    Blue Bluff River Festival. October. Held each year at the Blue Bluff Recreation Area at Tenn-Tom Waterway, the River Festival offers family fun: children's activities, food, live music, and arts and crafts. (662) 369-9440; (800) 634-3538.

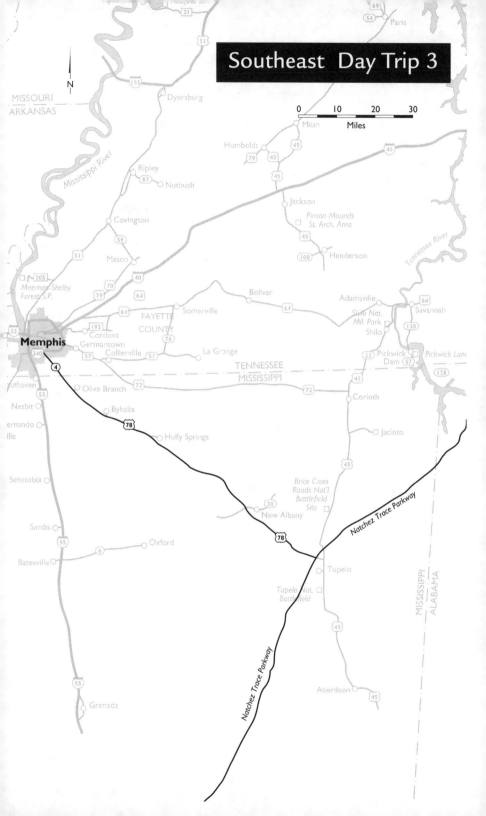

Southeast Day Trip 3

MISSOURI
ARKANSAS

N

Dyersburg

Milan

Miles

0   10   20   30

Humboldt

Ripley

Nutbush

Jackson

Pinson Mounds
St. Arch. Area

Covington

Henderson

Mason

Meeman-Shelby
Forest S.P.

Bolivar

Adamsville

Somerville

Shilo Nat.
Mil. Park

Savannah

Shilo

FAYETTE
COUNTY

Cordova
Germantown
Collierville

La Grange

Pickwick
Dam

Pickwick Land

Memphis

TENNESSEE
MISSISSIPPI

Olive Branch

Corinth

outhaven

Nesbit

Byhalia

ernando
ille

Holly Springs

Jacinto

Senatobia

Brice Cross
Roads Nat'l.
Battlefield
Site

New Albany

Sardis

Oxford

Batesville

Tupelo

Tupelo Nat.
Battlefield

Natchez Trace Parkway

MISSISSIPPI
ALABAMA

Grenada

Natchez Trace Parkway

Aberdeen

Natchez Trace Parkway, MS

NATCHEZ TRACE PARKWAY

The Natchez Trace Parkway is about a two-hour drive from Memphis. Take US 78 south, past New Albany about 25 miles. You can pick up the parkway going northeast toward Nashville or southwest toward Natchez, Mississippi. Tupelo makes a convenient town for an overnight stay; see Southeast Day Trip 2.

Between 1780 and 1830 the Natchez Trace had considerable significance for both military and commercial purposes. Native Americans first cleared the trail, and in the eighteenth century European settlers used it for travel and trade. Especially important for traders was its northern route. While American frontiersmen could ship goods south to New Orleans by way of the Mississippi River, they required a trail to carry goods north from Natchez to Nashville. Eventually, when settlers began moving into the Old Southwest, the Natchez Trace moved in both directions. By 1800 the army began developing the trail, and it became a post road. For many years the trace represented a distinct and valuable route in the American South, and many significant people crossed and traveled it, including Andrew Jackson in the War of 1812 and the great explorer Meriwether Lewis, of Lewis and Clark. In the early 1800s steamboats made the Natchez Trace obsolete—it was no longer needed to move goods and travelers north.

In 1938 the trail was officially designated the Natchez Trace Parkway, and it's now under the administration of the National Park Service. One of the tasks of the park service is to preserve the many historical monuments along the trace, including Emerald Mound, the second largest ceremonial mound in the United States, and a historic housing site, which was sponsored by President Roosevelt's New Deal. Other historical sites on the parkway include plantations, outposts, smaller ceremonial mounds, archaeological sites of uncovered villages, pioneer stands, and cemeteries.

The modern parkway, part of the National Scenic Byways Program, allows travelers to enjoy a relaxed drive (the speed limit is 50 miles per hour) through Mississippi, Alabama, and Tennessee, while absorbing both important American history and a beautiful, natural landscape. All but 20 miles of the 450-mile route between Natchez and Nashville is official parkway, and you can pick it up just outside Tupelo. In addition to visiting the historical sites and displays, travelers can stop at fifteen interpretive locations, as well as many granite mileposts describing points of interest and park services. In addition, there are many resting spots with scenic overlooks and picnic areas.

Although there are occasional deer on the road (drive carefully), no commercial vehicles are allowed on the parkway, and there are no restaurants, gas stations, or hotels. These modern conveniences (and necessities) are, however, available in neighboring towns. In fact, because travelers often like to make a weekend trip of the trace, an independent company has established a lodging reservation system: the Natchez Trace Bed-and-Breakfast Reservation Service. For information and accommodations, call (615) 285–2777; (800) 377–2770.

If you do intend to spend time out of your car and on the actual trail, you'll find a plethora of activities, including picnicking, hiking, and biking. Biking has become such a popular activity along the Natchez Trace that the Tennessee Department of Transportation publishes a map of the "Heartland" bike route. Call (615) 741–2848 for a copy. The Natchez Trace information line (601–680–4025 or 800–305–7417) can also supply you with information about biking routes, campgrounds, and other activities. If you're hiking and/or biking on the trails, be cautious of the fire ants, snakes, and poison ivy.

SOUTHAVEN

Just get yourself onto the southern loop of I-240 to take I-55 south toward Jackson, Mississippi. The drive to Southaven is a straight shot and takes only about fifteen minutes. You'll want to take exit 291 for Stateline Road, which puts you smack dab in Southaven, otherwise known as the Top of Mississippi and the former home of author John Grisham. You'll also be in De Soto County, named for the Spanish explorer Hernando de Soto, who traveled the area back in 1539. Some other—less famous—county locals are buried in the old Edmonson Cemetery on Stateline Road. A stroll through the grounds reveals the final resting place of Anna Leigh McCorkle, author of *Tales of Old Whitehaven*.

Though there's not a whole lot to do in this slow southern town, there's golf to be played here and in neighboring towns. Memphians make the trip to the greens at North Creek in Southaven as well as other popular courses in Olive Branch weekly. If you're not a golfer, just cruise on over to Cowboy Corner or the Harley shop; even if you're not a cowboy or a biker, you'll be both entertained and drawn in to the authentic and fun merchandise. For a springtime trip, head to Southaven in April, when Springfest, rated among the top twenty events in the Southeast by *Southern Living* magazine, is in full swing.

WHERE TO GO

Southaven Chamber of Commerce. 8700 Northwest Drive, Southaven, MS 36871. Southaven's chamber can provide you with

89

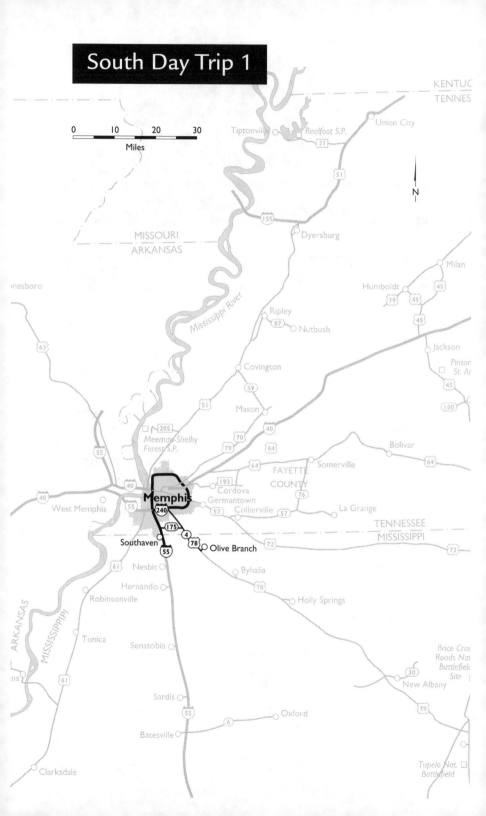

South Day Trip 1

```
0        10       20       30
|——|——|——|——|——|——|——|
         Miles
```

N

KENTUC
TENNES

Tiptonville
Reelfoot S.P.
Union City
21

51

155
Dyersburg

MISSOURI
ARKANSAS

nesboro

Milan

Humboldt
79   45
45

63

Ripley
87   Nutbush

45

Jackson

Pinson
St. A
45

Covington

59

100

51
Mason

70
64

Bolivar

205
79   64   Somerville   64
Meeman-Shelby
Forest S.P.   193
55   Cordova   FAYETTE
40   Germantown   COUNTY
                                         76
Memphis   57   Collierville 57   La Grange

240

West Memphis 55   TENNESSEE
                                                         MISSISSIPPI
175
4   72   72
78
Southaven   Olive Branch
55
                                         Byhalia
Nesbit
                                         78
Hernando
Robinsonville   Holly Springs

ARKANSAS
MISSISSIPPI
61
Tunica

Senatobia   Brice Cros
                                         Roads Nat
                                         Battlefiel
                                         Site
                                         30
                                         New Albany

Sardis
55
6   Oxford

Batesville   78

Clarksdale   Tupelo Nat.
                                         Battlefield

maps and information about the area. Open Monday through Friday. (662) 342-6365.

North Creek Golf Club. 8770 North Creek Boulevard, Southaven, MS 38671. This is a semiprivate eighteen-hole links-style par-seventy-two golf course with public play. Golfers are challenged with woods, water, rolling hills, dunes, and bunkers. On holes thirteen and fifteen, there's even a signature double green (the cart path tunnels beneath). The fairways are bermuda grass and the course, bentgrass. On every cart is a ProLink GPS yardage system, which calculates distance with a color monitor. In 1999 *Golf Digest* rated North Creek one of the best new courses in the country. For eighteen holes, the cost is $25 on weekdays, slightly higher on weekends; nine holes is about half the price. Cart rental is $15. Stop in at the Grill at the double green for lunch. It's a steakhouse offering salads, sandwiches, and, of course, steaks along with specialty menu items. There's also a full bar. □. (662) 280-4653.

WHERE TO SHOP

Cowboy Corner. 3698 Goodman Road East, Southaven, MS 38671. Opened in 1957 and occupying 16,000 square feet, Cowboy Corner is one of the oldest and largest western and saddlery stores in the South. Here you'll find everything western you could possibly want or imagine and probably hundreds of things you *never* imagined or thought you needed. Charles and Teresa Tackett, along with their family, own and manage the store and will help you sort through the variety of goods to find the perfect riding boots or leather saddle. For serious cowboys, Cowboy Corner offers a huge selection of saddles, many with ornate metal designs, an equally vast selection of tack and accessories. But amateur and wannabe cowboys should stop by to indulge their appetite for a genuine Stetson hat a la Clint Eastwood. Open seven days a week. □. www.thecowboycorner.com/. (662) 349-3267; (800) 748-8859.

Harley Davidson of De Soto County. 6935 Windchase Road, Horn Lake, MS 38637. The Web site calls this HD location a "state of the art store with good ole' down home service," and indeed, that's what you'll find. The employees really love Harleys, and they'll both educate you and reel you in: hook, line, and sinker. They have an impressive selection of bikes, which is worth a browse even if you're not a biker yourself. HD of De Soto also carries HD clothes, accessories, and children's items. To get to Horn Lake from Southaven, continue on I-55 south until you reach MS 302, exit 289. Closed Sunday. ☐. (662) 349-1099.

WHERE TO EAT

Avellino's. 775 Goodman Road East, Suite 7, Southaven, MS 38671. You want it, they got it. Avellino's has pizza, pasta, sub sandwiches, salads—too many things to list. It's open every day and will pack up a to-go meal, which is especially good for the nearby Olive Branch Old Towne concert series. $-$$; ☐. (662) 349-9968.

Boss Hog BBQ. 1092 Goodman Road East, Southaven, MS 38671. If you don't make it to Springfest in April to try Southaven's barbecue, stop in at Boss Hog's for a taste of Mississippi-style barbecue. You'll find the standard barbecue selection, with pork being the main menu item. $-$$; ☐. (662) 349-6573.

Dale's. 1226 Stateline Road West, Southaven, MS 38671. Dale's is simple and reliable, just like its name implies. It's southern-style, home-cooked food that'll remind you that you really are in Mississippi. Menu favorites include the fried pork chop and banana pudding. Yes, that's *fried pork chop.* $-$$; ☐. (662) 393-2060.

SPECIAL EVENTS

Springfest. April. Held every spring in honor of Southaven's incorporation in 1980, the three-day Springfest has become the most popular special event in the entire state of Mississippi. Each year 90,000 people participate in the festival's educational and cultural events, including live music, arts and crafts, and a barbecue contest, which serves as a preliminary contest for the Memphis in May BBQ Fest.

Southern Lights. December. With nearly 1.5 miles of holiday lights and displays, Southern Lights is Southaven-gone-Disney. Children, especially, love to watch the glowing Santas and sleighs with reindeer glide past as they cruise through the winter wonderland.

OLIVE BRANCH

Olive Branch is only a few minutes from Southaven. Go north on I-55 to TN 175 east; then exit south onto US 78 and drive southeast until you hit MS 305, where you'll head north into Olive Branch. If you want to skip the first stop on this day trip and come directly from Memphis, you can take Lamar Avenue due east, which turns into US 78 east. Centuries ago, the site of Olive Branch is where several old Chickasaw Indian trails crossed. Even the major thoroughfares like Old US 78/TN 178, once called Pigeon Roost Road, were well-traveled Indian trails. These days Olive Branch is the "nation's fastest growing city," according to the mayor's office, and has become a popular golf destination for both Memphians and visitors to the area. If you're not interested in golf, check out the famous bonsai nursery here and go home with a truly unique souvenir, or tour Old Towne to get a feel for how Olive Branch citizens lived years ago.

WHERE TO GO

Olive Branch Chamber of Commerce. 6820 Cockrum Street, Olive Branch, MS 38654. The town chamber can provide you with maps and information about the area. Open Monday through Friday. (662) 895-2600.

Brussel's Bonsai Nursery. 8365 Center Hill Road, Olive Branch, MS 38654. Brussel Martin opened this nursery back in 1972. It's now the premier bonsai nursery in all fifty United States. Brussel sells every kind of bonsai (miniature tree) imaginable, from the basic ficus to the more extraordinary ginkgo and juniper varieties. You can come home with a unique plant—and instructions for the novice bonsai owner—for less than $30. If you're a real arborist, plan your trip for Memorial Day weekend, when Brussel's hosts Rendezvous, a barbecue and bonsai fest. In addition to the great food, you can hear lectures on bonsai, participate in workshops, and watch demonstrations from bonsai artists as they create beautiful visions. Open weekdays and occasional Saturdays as weather permits (call ahead). ☐. www.brusselsbonsai.com. (662) 895-7457; (800) 582-2593.

Olive Branch City Park. 8257 Goodman Road, Olive Branch, MS 38654. The OB—as it's called by locals—makes a fun respite on a family day trip. There's the standard park fare: picnic areas with pavilions and grills, lighted walking trails, a playground, an outdoor amphitheater, and tennis courts. If you go on the weekend, you're liable to find a softball tournament in full swing: There are three enormous softball complexes comprised of twelve playing fields. (662) 895-4131.

Old Towne. 9189 Pigeon Roost Avenue, Olive Branch, MS 38654. Located in the center of Olive Branch, Old Towne is just what it sounds like: the oldest part of the city. It's a triangular commercial area nestled between "new" and "old" US 78. Locals say it's "two miles and a hundred years from Memphis." Although it's primarily a business and shopping district with several antiques and gift shops, the Old Towne Preservation Association works to bring community activities and celebrations here. For example, every spring and fall Old Towne hosts a live concert series, which attracts locals and visitors with picnics and lawn chairs in tow. Even on days when nothing special is planned, Old Towne makes a nice spot for an afternoon stroll. (662) 893-5012.

Cherokee Valley Golf Club. 6635 Crumpler Avenue, Olive Branch, MS 38654. There are some die-hard Cherokee Valley Golf lovers in Memphis who frequently make the trip to this eighteen-hole par-seventy-two bentgrass public course with water in play. From the driving range, you can hit from both mats and grass. Designed by Don Cottle Jr., it's a fairly new course, built in 1996. For $37 on a weekday, nonmembers can play eighteen holes; on weekends the price goes up to $46. And nine holes go for just under $20. Green fees include gas cart rental. If you're interested in something new, try Cherokee's twilight golfing. Call up to five days ahead for tee times. □. (662) 893-4444.

Plantation Golf. 9425 Plantation Road, Olive Branch, MS 38654. Golfers who play Plantation go there as much for the view as for the game. It's a beautiful, sweeping eighteen-hole par-seventy-two course with well-placed berms and thirty-five acres of water. Plantation has been host to numerous tournaments, such as the Jordan Mini-Tour, the True-Temper Classic, and the Michelob Tour America. Facilities include a pro shop, snack bar, driving range, and putting green. Rates are just under $40 for eighteen holes on the weekend, and slightly lower on weekdays. □. Tee times (901) 525-2411; clubhouse (662) 895-3530.

WHERE TO SHOP

Old Towne. Olive Branch residents claim that the Old Towne district is the antiques and gift shop capital of the Midsouth. With around twenty stores in this central locale, they're probably right. Start at these three shops on Pigeon Roost Road and work your way around the triangle:

All in the Family Gifts and Collectibles. 9128 Pigeon Roost Road, Olive Branch, MS 38654. (662) 893–6783.

Old Towne Antiques and Gifts. 9117 Pigeon Roost Road, Olive Branch, MS 38654. (662) 893–2323.

The Olive Branch Bazaar. 9119 Pigeon Roost Road, Olive Branch, MS 38654. (662) 895–9496.

The Gin. 7079 Depot Street, Olive Branch, MS 38654. If you've shopped the antiques stores and gift boutiques in Old Towne proper, venture the block and a half to the Gin, as in *cotton gin*. What you miraculously didn't find in the triangle, you'll find at the Gin, a marketplace stuffed full of every home accessory imaginable. Maggie O'Hara's is the all-time favorite among the shops in Olive Branch's most unusual shopping emporium.

WHERE TO EAT

Oasis Grill and Shoe Shine Parlor. 9099 Old Highway 78, Olive Branch, MS 38654. Even among some of the oldest Olive Branch residents, no one seems to know why "Shoe Shine Parlor" is part of the name of this thirty-year-old town tradition. But no one seems to mind either. The Oasis is truly a community home-cooking restaurant with basic meals like burgers, sandwiches, and salads. Locals meet for coffee each morning and often grab lunch instead of staying home. It's just a two-block walk from Old Towne. Open Monday through Friday for all meals, and Saturday for breakfast only. $–$$; ☐. (662) 895–4554.

The Magnolia Café. 7465 Goodman Road, Olive Branch, MS 38654. Not far from the OB park is the Magnolia Café, which offers a changing selection every day. There's actually no menu, because it's always a buffet. Sometimes there's smoked turkey, sometimes brisket, sometimes red beans and rice, and sometimes mashed potatoes. But no matter which day you come, you're guaranteed a good home-cooked meal. $–$$. (662) 895–4460.

WHERE TO STAY

Whispering Woods Hotel and Conference Center. 11200 East Goodman Road, Olive Branch, MS 38654. If you want something a little different from the standard Hampton Inn, try Whispering Woods Hotel and Conference Center, which is located on 400 acres of secluded wooded property and is a bona fide golf resort. The hotel offers a choice of parlor suites and efficiencies. Guests enjoy a variety of activities in the various hotel facilities, including a swimming pool, hot tub, sauna, game room, jogging track, fitness center, lighted tennis courts, and golf. There's also a restaurant on site. Children under seventeen stay free. $$; □. (662) 895-2941.

The Whispering Woods public golf course, designed by Clay Harrington and built in 1979, is adjacent to the hotel and features an eighteen-hole bermuda grass course with water in play. Green fees for nonmembers are $30 on weekends for eighteen holes, but it's half price Monday through Friday. Call ahead for tee times. Both gas and pull carts as well as clubs are available for rental. Golfers can enjoy a leisurely snack and drink at the nineteenth-hole lounge. □. (662) 895-3500.

SPECIAL EVENTS

May-Fest. May. About a hundred arts and crafts vendors come to Olive Branch during May-Fest to sell and demonstrate their wares. The fun takes place in Old Towne and includes activities, entertainment, and food. (662) 893-5012

Spring Concert Series. Mid-May–mid-June. Every Thursday at 7:00 P.M., music lovers flock to Old Towne for the Spring Concert Series, which features a variety of live music. Bring a chair and picnic.

Old Tyme Festival. June. In addition to food and musical entertainment, the Old Tyme Festival includes a variety of activities, such as pony rides, a Civil War reenactment, arts and crafts, and children's games. (662) 429-3609.

Fall Concert Series. Mid-September–mid-October. The Spring Concert Series is so popular that come September, Old Towne hosts another series. Every Saturday at 7:00 P.M.

Octoberfest. October. Held at the Olive Branch City Park, Octoberfest is your basic but fun family festival, including children's games, pony rides, a petting zoo, a fishing rodeo, food, entertainment, and arts and crafts. (662) 895–5448.

Old Towne Street Rod Run. October. Everything happens in October in Olive Branch, including the Rod Run, when the Old Towne district is blocked off to traffic and about seventy-five street rodders exhibit their early-twentieth-century antique cars. There are plenty of activities, entertainment, and food. (662) 893–5012.

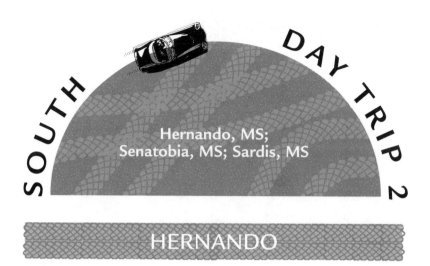

SOUTH

DAY TRIP 2

Hernando, MS;
Senatobia, MS; Sardis, MS

HERNANDO

To reach Hernando, Mississippi, you simply follow I-55 south. Once you cross the Mississippi border, it won't be long until you reach the home of two of the most intimate bed-and-breakfasts in the South. The history of Hernando is fascinating. Located only a few miles away from Memphis is the site of Mississippi's oldest county seat. Built in 1866, the county courthouse has become quite famous, as it has been featured in a number of motion pictures. Inside the courthouse features a number of murals portraying the travels of the city's namesake and famous Spanish conquistador, Hernando de Soto, who first visited the area in 1541.

WHERE TO STAY

Sassafras Inn Bed and Breakfast. 785 Highway 51, Hernando, MS 38632. Situated in a serene country setting, the Sassafras Inn is an English Tudor–style bed-and-breakfast built in 1985. Because of the quiet atmosphere, Sassafras Inn boasts being a "haven away from daily cares." The grounds include an indoor pool, tropical gardens, waterfalls, and a hot tub. Large breakfasts are served daily, and you can enjoy your breakfast in a variety of settings—from the formal dining room to the patio, or even in the privacy of your room. All guest rooms in the main house feature queen-sized beds, a large private bath, cable TV, a VCR, a CD

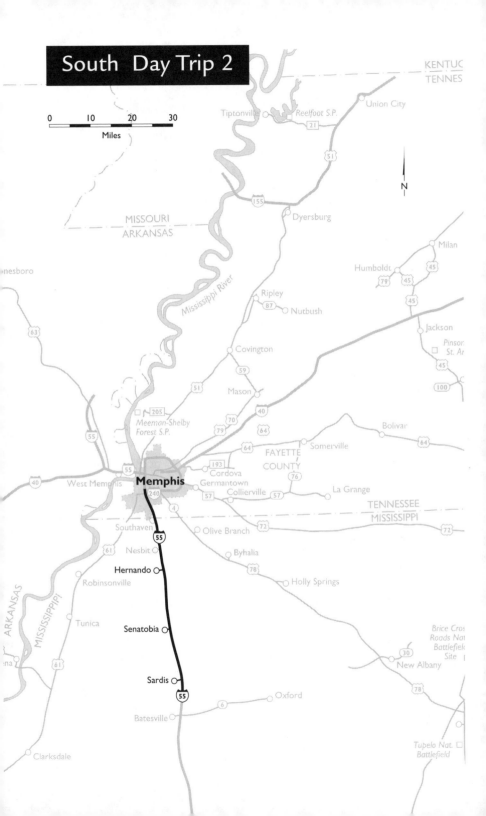

South Day Trip 2

0   10   20   30
Miles

N

KENTUC
TENNES

Tiptonville
Reelfoot S.P.
21
Union City

51

MISSOURI
ARKANSAS

155

Dyersburg

Milan

Humboldt
79
45
45

nesboro

Mississippi River

Ripley
87
Nutbush

63

Jackson

Pinson
St. Ar

45

Covington

59

100

Mason

51

205

70
40

Meeman-Shelby
Forest S.P.

79
64

Bolivar

64

55

64
US 64
Somerville

FAYETTE
COUNTY

64

40
West Memphis

55

Memphis

240

193
Cordova
Germantown
57
Collierville
57
76
La Grange

TENNESSEE
MISSISSIPPI

4

Southaven

55

Olive Branch
72

72

61
Nesbit

Byhalia

78

Hernando

Robinsonville

Holly Springs

Brice Cros
Roads Nat
Battlefield
Site

Senatobia

30
New Albany

ARKANSAS
MISSISSIPPI

Tunica

na
61

Sardis

55

6
Oxford

78

Batesville

Clarksdale

Tupelo Nat.
Battlefield

music player, and robes. Some of the more popular guest rooms overlook the indoor pool. For a romantic getaway, couples can stay in the Heart's Content Cottage, with its winding sidewalk and lit bridge. The cottage features a private hot tub, rice bed with canopy top, robes, refrigerator, color TV, VCR, built-in stereo system, and breakfast in bed.

Activities abound at Sassafras Inn. Guests can sit and swing leisurely under an oak tree or enjoy a lively game of billiards. The inn also features a home theater where you can relax and watch a movie or select a movie from the video library to watch in your room. $$-$$$; □. (662) 429-5864.

Magnolia Grove. 140 East Commerce Street, Hernando, MS 38632. Nestled on three acres and amid a number of magnolia trees is Magnolia Grove bed-and-breakfast, built in the 1900s. This Greek Revival mansion typifies southern charm with its two-story portico, columns, and porte cochere on the outside, along with a stately staircase, towering 12-foot ceilings, and chandeliers inside. Although turn of the twentieth century in feel, Magnolia Grove's lodging accommodations leave nothing to be desired for modern-day travelers. Select from four ornate guest rooms—the Rose Room, Ladye Magnolia, Golfer's Haven, and Cole's Cottage. Innkeeper Phyllis Wolf serves extravagant gourmet breakfasts, and dinners can be prepared with a reservation. Be sure to pick up a copy of *Favorite Recipes from Magnolia Grove Bed and Breakfast* so you can remember this charming stop long after you've returned home. $$$; □. (662) 429-2626.

Brigadoon Farm Retreat. 350 Highway 305 South, Hernando, MS 38654. Near the Coldwater River, the Brigadoon combines rustic and modern to create a relaxing resort getaway. There are eleven rooms at the inn, six with private bath, and a separate guest cottage and large log cabin on the premises. The farm retreat's facilities include a playground, sitting room, restaurant, swimming pool, hot tubs, a picnic area, and a lake, complete with fishing and complimentary pedal boats. If you're up for some exercise, try the Brigadoon's hiking and biking trails. And if it's hunting season, you can even hunt here. Innkeeper Jeanette Martin provides all her guests with complimentary wine, three meals each day, snacks, and afternoon tea. Children are welcome, but no pets. Closed in January. $$-$$$; □. (662) 895-3098; (877) 895-3098.

SPECIAL EVENTS

Christmas in Dixie Tour of Antebellum Homes. December. Annually, five historic homes in De Soto County are selected for touring. For more information, times, and locations, please contact the chamber of commerce at (662) 429-4414.

SENATOBIA

From Hernando, continue south on I-55 for 15 miles to reach Senatobia. Once you're there, you'll want to stop off at the Spahn House, an inn where you'll be treated like royalty.

WHERE TO SHOP

Rita's Petites. 100 North Front Street, Senatobia, MS 38668. Rita opened this shop in 1984 out of the sheer frustration of not being able to find clothes to fit the shorter woman. Today Rita's Petites features fine clothes from makers like Kasper, Eileen Fisher, Sigrid Olsen, Cynthia Max, Nancy Bolen, Marisa Christina, and Susan Bristol. Open from 9:30 A.M. to 5:30 P.M. Monday through Friday, and Saturday from 10:00 A.M. to 4:00 P.M. (662) 562-7602.

WHERE TO STAY

Spahn House. 401 College Street, Senatobia, MS 38668. Spahn House, built in 1904 in the Neoclassical style, is a gracious fifteen-room southern mansion situated on a picture-perfect shady street. Beautifully restored and decorated with fine antiques, Spahn House offers all the charm and comfort of traditional southern hospitality. Call at least two days in advance to discuss your menus with the innkeepers. That way, you can plan your meals right down to the salad dressing before you arrive. Dinner is served in the formal dining room and is private. At $100 per couple, it's the perfect treat for a special occasion. If you really want to go all out, take advantage of the Romance Package, which includes two white terry robes, roses, candles, champagne, and dinner served with crystal, silver, and linen ($45 extra).

The inn features four inviting and individually decorated guest rooms. With a Jacuzzi bath for two and color TV in each room, you can rest in complete comfort and privacy. In the morning you're served a breakfast fit for royalty along with a copy of the local paper. Spahn House can also be very accommodating for special occasions and events. Private corporate dinners, anniversaries, honeymoons, and private candlelight dinners for two are specialties. The inn provides a wonderful setting for luncheons, weddings, and receptions as well. $$–$$$; ☐. (662) 562-9853.

SARDIS

Continue along I-55 south toward Jackson, Mississippi. Take the MS 315 exit (exit 252) toward Sardis. Turn right onto MS 315. When you arrive at Sardis, you've reached one of the best fishing holes in all of Mississippi as well as one of the most peaceful, laid-back communities in the area with a population of about 2,100.

WHERE TO GO

Sardis Chamber of Commerce. 114 West Lee Street, Sardis, MS 38666. Stop by the chamber to grab maps and directions before heading to the lake. You can also get the scoop on what's going on around town. (662) 487-3451.

Mallard Pointe Golf Course. 3037 State Park Road, Sardis, MS 38666. Built in 1997, this eighteen-hole public course designed by architect Bob Cupp is located within John Kyle State Park; it's a spectacular course worth the drive from Memphis. Striking elevation changes abound at this track, which measures 6,500 yards from the back tees. Cupp also added a nine-hole short course perfect for practicing the elusive short game, or for that quick afternoon round after work.

Mallard Pointe's clubhouse offers equipment, food, and a place to relax after your round. Add the amenities available at John Kyle State Park and you can provide any size group with a golf event of any size. (662) 487-2400.

John W. Kyle State Park. Route 1, Box 115, Sardis, MS 38666. Recreational offerings include 58,500-acre Sardis Reservoir, a swimming pool, tennis courts, a recreation building, twenty cabin units, group camp housing for 150, and a 200-site campground on Sardis Lower Lake with adjacent swimming beaches and nature trails. (662) 487-1345.

Sardis Lake. Scenic Loop 315, Sardis, MS 38666. This reservoir provides numerous recreational activities, including fishing, hunting, camping, and boating. Sardis Lake is a vital part of the Yazoo Basin Flood Control System, which protects downstream agricultural and industrial areas. While the lake itself runs through three Mississippi counties, the dam is located in Sardis; it became functional in 1940. Hunters can roam through a wide variety of landscapes, including hardwood forests, pine plantations, open fields, and wetlands, as they search out deer, squirrels, quail, turkeys, doves, and a variety of waterfowl. Anglers will find a multitude of crappies, bass, and catfish within the waters of the lake. At the end of a full day of hunting, fishing, or boating, visitors can rest at the lake's camping area. Designated tent and trailer sites come with electrical hookups, rest rooms and bathhouses, picnic tables and grills. If you're new to the area or just want to be filled in on all the lake has to offer, attend one of the presentations held by park rangers at the Oak Grove amphitheater or at the Clear Springs trail area. The lecture includes discussion on the area's wildlife and history. (662) 487-1345.

SPECIAL EVENTS

Wizard of Oz Children's Theatre Camp. July. Panola Playhouse, P.O. Box 43, Sardis, MS 38666. Sponsored by the Panola Playhouse, this camp gives children ages six to fourteen the opportunity to learn all about theater production, including acting, direction, makeup, sets, props, lighting, and scenery. The camp lasts for three weeks and ends with a play performance that demonstrates what the children have learned at the camp. There's an admission fee for the performance. (662) 487-3975.

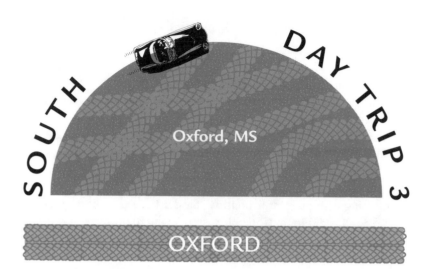

SOUTH DAY TRIP 3

Oxford, MS

OXFORD

Home of Ole Miss and Faulkner's mansion, tailgate parties, and literary readings, Oxford, Mississippi, is South with a capital *S*. It's a little over an hour's drive from Memphis, south along I-55 and east on MS 6. Leaving the busy interstate and turning onto the state road, you'll see the requisite fast-food restaurants for a quick break and the only outlet strip mall for hundreds of miles. It's the last stop before your journey back in time and sensibility. Continue east on MS 6 for about twenty minutes to Oxford, where the local farms, vegetable stands, and used-truck lots that speckle the northern Mississippi border give way to the sprawl of the University of Mississippi campus, known to natives as Ole Miss.

This intimate and unassuming town has been called "a thriving New South Arts Mecca" by *USA Today*. And it truly is a hub of cultural activity, sponsored primarily by the university and inspired by Oxford's most famous citizen, William Faulkner. There's a lot to do here: fabulous boutique shopping around the square, educational but entertaining exhibits at Ole Miss, fine and casual dining, and, of course, Rowan Oak and all the other tidbits that gave us Faulkner's Yoknapatawpha County. Because Oxford is about an hour and a half from Memphis, you can make your trip in one day, but the distance also makes this a great overnight trip: It's just far enough away with such charming inns that it's well worth the splurge for a guest room.

104

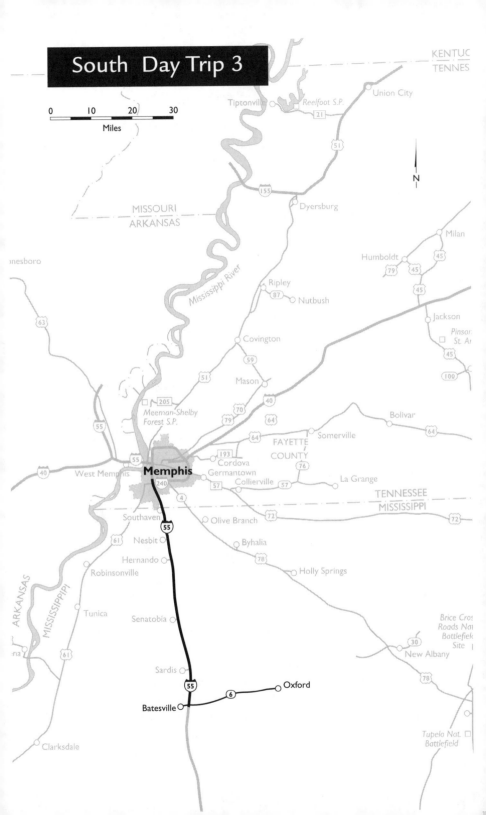

South Day Trip 3

0   10   20   30
Miles

KENTUC
TENNES

Tiptonville   Reelfoot S.P.   Union City

21

Reelfoot S.P.

51

155

N

MISSOURI
ARKANSAS

Dyersburg

Milan

nesboro

Humboldt   45

79   45

63

Ripley

45

87   Nutbush

Mississippi River

Jackson

Pinson
St. A

Covington

59

45

100

51

Mason

70

40

64

Bolivar

205

79

64   FAYETTE   Somerville   64

Meeman-Shelby
Forest S.P.

COUNTY

55

193

Cordova

76

Memphis

Germantown

La Grange

240   Collierville   57

40

West Memphis

57

TENNESSEE
MISSISSIPPI

Southaven

4

72

55

72

61

Olive Branch

Nesbit

Byhalia

ARKANSAS

Hernando

78

Robinsonville

Holly Springs

Tunica

Brice Cros
Roads Na
Battlefiel
Site

MISSISSIPPI

Senatobia

30

New Albany

61

Sardis

55

78

6   Oxford

Batesville

Clarksdale

Tupelo Nat.
Battlefield

WHERE TO GO

Oxford Tourism Council. 111 Courthouse Square, Oxford, MS 38655. Stop in at the conveniently located Oxford tourist office to collect maps and information about this college town. Open weekdays. (662) 234-4680; (800) 758-9177.

Driving tour. Oxford, MS. Weaving your way through Oxford toward its center is both necessary and worthwhile, and it's easy if you just follow the signs to Courthouse Square. The local residential architecture and the campus itself represent historic southern aesthetics and contemporary student life, respectively. Oxford has all the hustle and bustle of good old-fashioned college life suffused in southern gentility. All in all, it's a comfortable and familiar setting in which to enjoy an hour meandering leisurely through the narrow, tree-lined streets.

Courthouse Square. Oxford, MS. While in Oxford, orient yourself by the town square: It's classic in style and central in locale. Wherever you go, you'll always be able to find your way back; signs abound pointing you in the right direction. In the center of the square is the Lafayette County Courthouse, and all around it are exactly the things you'd expect: clothing boutiques, antiques shops, restaurants, bookstores, and pubs. Square Books and City Grocery, on the east corner, are perhaps the best known of Oxford's local businesses and draw customers from hundreds of miles away. Just take a stroll around the square and let the shops beckon you. This little pocket of culture is so consuming that by the end of the day you'll agree with the popular local poster that reads THE SQUARE IS THE CENTER OF THE UNIVERSE.

Rowan Oak. Oxford, MS 38655. If you want to add some literary history to your day trip, take the thirty-minute walk from the town square up to Faulkner's former home, Rowan Oak, which is, incidentally, so well known that it doesn't have—or need—an actual address. Again, just follow the signs from the square to get you there. For a small donation, you can tour the mansion and the grounds and sense for yourself the grandeur and mysticism so central to Faulkner's Yoknapatawpha County novels. Be sure to spend some time in the writer's spare office, where he outlined the plot of *A Fable* on the wall. If you're lucky, the host will allow you to step past the rope and into the kitchen hall to see the phone where Faulkner heard he'd won the Nobel Prize. Open Tuesday through Saturday and Sunday afternoon. (662) 234-3284.

The University of Mississippi Museums. Fifth and University Avenues, Oxford, MS 38655. After your tour of Faulkner's Rowan Oak, you can take the path through Bailey's Woods to Ole Miss's museum complex. The collections include Greek and Roman antiquities, nineteenth-century scientific instruments, southern folk art, and works of Mississippi painter Theora Hamblett. The museum also hosts a variety of educational programs and tours for adults and children. (662) 915-7073.

Blues Archive. Farley Hall, University of Mississippi, Oxford, MS 38655. The Blues Archive at Ole Miss is the most extensive collection of blues recordings and artifacts in the world. There are three main collections: the B. B. King Collection, which has more than 7,000 recordings, films, and photos; the Kenneth S. Goldstein Folklore Collection, displaying African American music and folklore in the form of books, journals, and records; and the Living Blues Archive Collection, which consists of a wide variety of materials (posters, tapes, photos, books) covering the blues. Free admission; open weekdays. (662) 915-7091.

The Center for the Study of Southern Culture. Grove Circle and Sorority Row, University of Mississippi, Oxford, MS 38655. Although the Center for the Study of Southern Culture was established in 1977 primarily as an academic resource center for scholars of the South, it does occasionally exhibit interesting collections of both historical and contemporary southern arts and crafts. The exhibits are open to the public, as are occasional musical events, dramatic readings, performances, and films. The center is housed in the Barnard Observatory, one of only three surviving antebellum buildings on Ole Miss's campus. (662) 915-5993.

WHERE TO SHOP

Nielson's Department Store. 119 Courthouse Square, Oxford, MS 38655. Nielson's—pronounced like "Nelson's"—has been around for more than 150 years, making it the oldest store in town. The memorabilia on the back wall of the customer service area testifies to this fact: There's a letter from Faulkner and numerous antique photos of the store. Nielson's is a full-service department store, selling clothing and accessories for him and her, as well as accessories for the home. □. (662) 234-1161.

Southside Gallery. 150 Courthouse Square, Oxford, MS 38655. Southside is one of several charming art galleries on the square. With contemporary paintings, prints, sculpture, and photography, it has something for everyone. □. (662) 234-9090.

Square Books. 160 Courthouse Square, Oxford, MS 38655. Square Books is really more than a bookstore; it's the intellectual gathering spot of Oxford. In addition to two floors filled to capacity with every book imaginable and a hip, happening coffee bar, Square has a frequent and fun reading series, which hosts writers from all over the country as well as local authors. The most famous living author from Oxford is John Grisham, and Square is one of only two bookstores in the country where Grisham will read from and sign his books. Browse through the incredible array of books and then wander upstairs to enjoy a cup of java and listen to the writers read their work aloud to a captive audience. □. www2.squarebooks.com. (662) 236-2262.

LeShea's. 138 Courthouse Square, Oxford, MS 38655. You'll find everything you need at LeShea's, the town's be-all antiques, apparel, gift, cosmetics, and art boutique. Best known for its exquisite antique furnishings and objets d'art (porcelain and pottery), this shop caters to Oxford's small-town but sophisticated gentility. No matter what you're looking for, chances are you can find it here among the beaded purses, turquoise earrings, embroidered sweaters, chiffon scarves, candles, and framed paintings. □. (662) 236-5741.

AC's Bed and Bath Company. 138 Courthouse Square, Oxford, MS 38655. Even though it's not a spa, AC's makes you feel like you've been to one. Walking through this shop is like getting a good dose of aromatherapy. Candles, soaps, bath salts, even linens and bath accessories adorn the intimate setting of this tranquil spot. Take a breather from the hustle and bustle of the town square by stepping in and finding a gift for a friend or yourself. Favorite items at AC's include crushed velvet pillows, sateen sheets, and French body lotion. □. (662) 234-3753.

WHERE TO EAT

Ajax Diner. 118 Courthouse Square, Oxford, MS 38655. You can get pretty much anything at Ajax, but the menu items to order are the red bean (egg) rolls, the crawfish pie, the fried oyster po' boy, and the hot tamale pie. If you ask for tea, the waitress will bring you sweet. Ajax is southern cooking at its most southern. But if you're really just looking for burger or a steak, you'll find menu basics, too. All in all, you can't miss at this hometown diner. ☐. (662) 232-8880

City Grocery. 152 Courthouse Square, Oxford, MS 38655. This casual fine-dining restaurant offers a fabulous and sometimes eccentric array of delicacies, and the menu changes along with the seasons. One autumn list included crawfish and roasted corn cakes, spinach and duck confit, cassoulet of rabbit and tasso ham, bourbon-marinated grilled chicken, and herb-steamed salmon medallions. If you see the fried oyster salad on your menu, get it. The restaurant has a full bar upstairs and boasts an impressive wine list, with about thirty wines offered by the glass. In nice weather the manager opens the French doors onto the square itself and allows you to people-watch from the comfort of your white-clothed table and cozy candlelit ambience. Many Memphians drive to Oxford just for City Grocery's fare, so call ahead for reservations. $$$; ☐. (662) 232-8080.

Old Venice Pizza Company. 1112 Van Buren Avenue, Oxford, MS 38655. A favorite among Ole Miss students and townspeople alike, OVPC is the pizza stronghold of Oxford and just off the square. This casual joint has all the standard Italian cuisine, including lasagna and hand-tossed pizza, but adds a continental flair with entrees like the Chung Pao and Crawdad Delight angel-hair pastas. $$; ☐. (662) 234-OVPC.

Proud Larry's Restaurant and Spirits. 211 South Lamar Boulevard, Oxford, MS 38655. Proud Larry's is located just south of Courthouse Square along Lamar, and it's the perfect spot if you're looking for something laid back and rowdy. The menu has everything from a traditional Caesar salad to spicy Creole catfish and hearty pasta Bolognese, and all for less than $10. Most nights, and some afternoons, Larry's hosts local and regional bands, many of whom favor the easy pace of reggae. $-$$; ☐. (662) 236-0050.

WHERE TO STAY

Downtown Inn. 400 North Lamar Boulevard, Oxford, MS 38655. The 200-room inn—a former Holiday Inn— is just 100 feet from the square, making it the best spot to stay for easy access to the shops and restaurants. Though in a prime commercial location, the inn is also adjacent to a residential neighborhood, which means you'll have a nice, quiet sleep. You can choose from a wide range of floor plans, including suites and standard or deluxe rooms. It's even pet-friendly. $$; □. (662) 234-3031.

Clear Creek Cottage. 810 Lincoln Avenue, Oxford, MS 38655. Located just eight minutes from Oxford proper, this three-bedroom, three-bath cottage totaling 2,500 square feet has views encompassing a lush pond and green pastures. It occupies a forty-five-acre private horse farm. Indoors, the cottage has high ceilings, an elegant sitting room, and a serene atmosphere. From the porch, guests can enjoy lemonade while they soak up the southern tranquility that pervades the scene. Clear Creek Cottage is also a favorite among hunters who stop in Oxford for the night. A full house of six guests comes to $300 daily; the proprietor prorates for fewer guests. $$-$$$. (662) 234-4388.

The Tree House. 53 Highway 321, Oxford, MS 38655. With five upstairs guest rooms and one ground-floor, handicapped-accessible bedroom (all with private bath), the Tree House bed-and-breakfast is both cozy and accommodating. Guests enjoy a full breakfast in the formal dining room and casual socializing with an afternoon glass of sangria in the living room. You know you're still south of the Mason Dixon line because the bedrooms have names like Bubba's Room and Auntie Em's Room.

This log cabin rests on five acres of woodlands only 4 miles from the center of Oxford and Ole Miss. From the square, turn onto South Lamar Boulevard; after 2.5 miles, turn right onto Highway 321. The Tree House is about 0.5 mile down the highway on your left. $$; □. www.thetreehousebandb.com/. (662) 513-6354

Oliver-Britt House Inn and Tea Room. 512 Van Buren Avenue, Oxford, MS 38655. For yet another Greek Revival experience, check in at the Oliver-Britt House, which is located between the campus and the square. It was built circa 1905 and offers guests a choice of five bedrooms, all with private bath, antique furnishings, and television. For weekday breakfast, you'll dine at Oxford's best spot for morning grub: Smitty's. But on weekends your hosts, Glynn Oliver and Mary Ann Britt, serve a traditional southern breakfast at the inn. $$; □. (662) 234-8043.

Puddin' Place Bed and Breakfast. 1008 University Avenue, Oxford, MS 38655. Your car can stay put in its parking spot all weekend if you slumber at Puddin' Place, which is right in the thick of things. Just off the square, this hundred-year-old B&B is a historic building with antiques throughout, though it has been restored with all the modern amenities: air-conditioning and ceiling fans for hot summer nights and TVs for lounging in your room, to name a few. As you walk through Puddin' Place, be sure to enjoy the collectibles and historic mementos. There are just two rooms, and children are welcome (though pets are not). Your cost for the night includes a full breakfast in the inn's dining room, compliments of your host, Ann Turnbow. $$-$$$; ☐. (601) 234-1250.

Worthy Guest House. 1301 Buchanan, Oxford, MS 38655. The Worthy Guest House is a nicely appointed home furnished with antiques. There are three rooms with private bath. The best part about the Worthy, though, is its owner and your host, Opal Worthy, a well-traveled retired university professor. She'll help plan your day trip in and around Oxford while offering personal stories of days gone by. $$. (601) 234-3310.

SPECIAL EVENTS

Double-decker Festival. April. Everything goes during Oxford's Double-decker on the square: great food, local arts and crafts, a sidewalk sale, live music, a children's fair.

GRENADA

Take US 55 south from Memphis to Grenada, Mississippi. This charming little town is undergoing some big changes, especially downtown. This small town had quite an unusual beginning. Its roots lie in a literal marriage between two dueling towns—Pittsburg and Tullahoma. The area was settled in the 1830s, and the two towns were separated by a surveyor's line, which is still marked today as Line Street. The plan to merge the two towns included marrying a bride and groom from each town, and finishing off the ceremony with a barbecue dinner. Unfortunately, before dinner was ever served, the people of Pittsburg became disgruntled by the selection of names for the new town. Finally, they agreed on Grenada, and the rest, as they say, is history.

WHERE TO GO

Grenada Tourism Commission. 1321 Sunset Drive, Grenada, MS 38901. Swing by the Grenada Tourism Commission to find out highlights about Grenada Lake and get maps of the trails. (662) 226-2571.

Cougar Haven. This sanctuary for exotic cats is home to more than twenty animals, including tigers, lions, and cougars. Owner David Mallory brought these cats from facilities that weren't able to care for them, and he has given them a safe haven for them to live each of their nine lives in a completely fulfilled style. Call in advance for directions and times. (662) 226-0746.

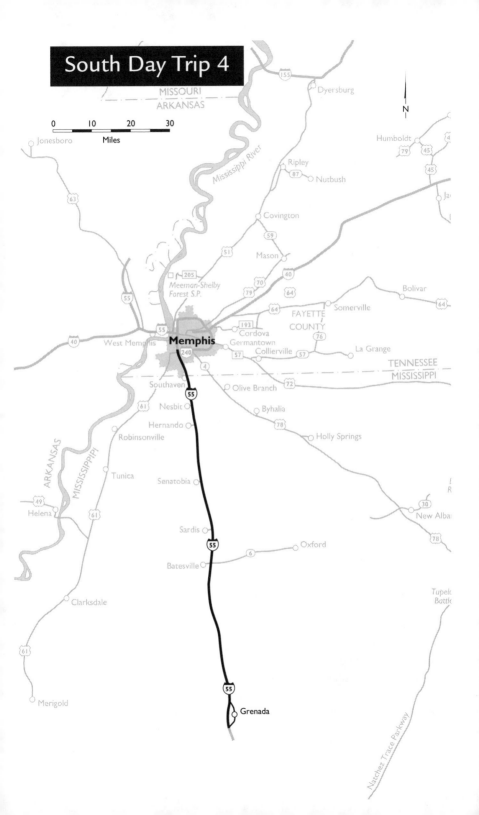

Lost Bluff Hiking Trail. Scenic Route 333, Grenada, MS 38901. This strenuous trail is 2 miles long and leads you through a wide variety of terrain. There are picturesque rest stops along the way, which provide several different scenic overlooks of Grenada Lake. (662) 226–1679.

Grenada Lake. Scenic Route 333, Grenada, MS 38901. Grenada Lake is a recreational delight. At more than 38,000 acres, it's the largest lake in Mississippi. Visitors can enjoy this reservoir while sailing, skiing, boating, or fishing. Don't miss the Grenada Lake and Visitor's Center, operated by the Corps of Engineers. Here you can see a video on the history of the lake and the construction of the dam, as well as tanks of local fish including crappies, bluegills, catfish, minnows, and bass. And take a step out onto the large observation deck that overlooks the reservoir. (662) 226–1679.

WHERE TO SHOP

Grenada Antique Mall and Bistro. 204 South Main Street, Grenada, Mississippi 38901. Owner Sheryl Putnam opened the mall in 2000 to escape her hectic Memphis life. She selected a historic Masonic lodge for the setting and spent months restoring the structure, which is on the National Register of Historic Places. When you step inside, you almost forget you're in a store—it's more like visiting an antebellum living room. This unique market is home to dozens of antiques dealers from Mississippi, Alabama, Louisiana, and Tennessee and features furniture, silver, crystal, as well as the works of local artisans. Putnam also carries unique papier-mâché mobiles from Seattle, Sid Dickens tiles from Canada, hand-monogrammed French linens, Peter's pottery and handcrafted bulletin boards made from old frames. The bistro features a wide variety of delectable dishes, and the menu changes regularly. (662) 226-8228.

First Street Gallery. 223 First Street, Grenada, MS 38901. The First Street Gallery started in 1998 with the support of the Grenada Main Street Association. It exhibits quality art and provides educational opportunities through visual arts and lectures. Housed in the historical Grenada Bank—constructed in the 1840s—the gallery has an extensive variety of local art available for both viewing and for purchase. The building itself was restored in the late 1970s and provides a glimpse into the architecture of the nineteenth century. Open daily. (662) 227-9349.

SPECIAL EVENTS

Lofton Archery Classic and U.S. Championship. May. This annual event held on Grenada Lake is the largest archery tournament in Mississippi. Of course, if you come as an onlooker, you won't be bored. There's more than just marksmanship on display here—you'll also find live entertainment, food, and archery equipment for sale. (800) 373-2571.

National Foxhunt Chase. October. Held at Graysport Landing on Grenada Lake, this event draws hunters from all around to follow the hounds in a chase for the cunning fox. In addition to foxhunting, guests can also watch bench shows and horse shows during this weeklong event. (800) 373-2571.

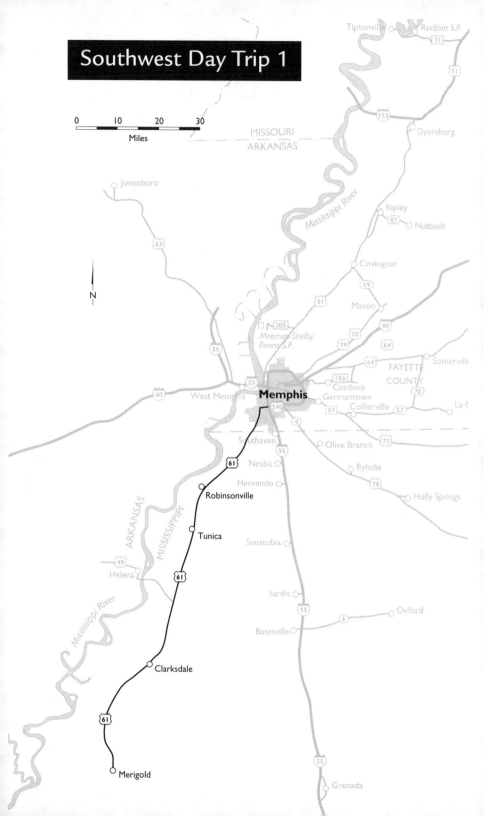

Southwest Day Trip 1

0   10   20   30
Miles

N

MISSOURI
ARKANSAS

Tiptonville
Reelfoot S.P.
21
51
155
Dyersburg

Jonesboro

Mississippi River

Ripley
87
Nutbush

63

Covington

59
51
Mason
40
205
70
79
64
Meeman-Shelby
Forest S.P.
64
FAYETTE
COUNTY
Somerville
76
55
193
Cordova
Germantown
57
Collierville
57
La C

Memphis
240
4
West Memphis
40

55

Southaven
55
Olive Branch
72
61
Nesbit
Byhalia

Hernando
78

Robinsonville
Holly Springs

Tunica
Senatobia

ARKANSAS
MISSISSIPPI
49
61
Helena
Sardis
55
Oxford
6
Batesville

Mississippi River

Clarksdale

61

55

Merigold
Grenada

TUNICA COUNTY: ROBINSONVILLE AND TUNICA

Tunica County is one of the most popular destinations in Mississippi, primarily because of the casinos. Nestled among quiet country roads is Robinsonville, home of the Midsouth's version of Las Vegas gaming. And further into Tunica County is the town of Tunica, a charming and quaint Mississippi hotspot. To reach Tunica County, you'll want to head toward downtown Memphis via Poplar Avenue and turn south on Third Street. After a few miles, Third Street changes into Route 61 south. Although most of the drive is peaceful, once you cross the county line, things are anything but quiet. The bright lights, big shows, and game tables of ten outstanding resorts beckon even the most reserved visitor.

Tunica hasn't always been the home of glitz and glamour. The town was settled along the Mississippi River during the heyday of the steamboat. Once the train became America's mode of commerce, the town of Tunica, which was chartered in 1888, packed up and headed for the railroad tracks. When you visit Tunica proper today, you'll notice how the town is laid out in a linear fashion on either side of the railroad.

WHERE TO GO

Tunica Chamber of Commerce. 1278 East Edwards Avenue, Tunica, MS 38676. There's a lot more to Tunica than just the casinos. Behind all the bright lights is a charming little town that welcomes visitors from all around the Midsouth. Stop by the chamber of commerce to get information on events and points of interest. (662) 363-2865.

Blues and Legends Hall of Fame. Horseshoe Casino, 1020 Casino Center Drive, Robinsonville, MS 38664. The Mississippi Delta is known for being the birthplace of the blues, so it's only fitting that this progressive southern town hosts a museum honoring the blues. The Blues and Legends Hall of Fame pays tribute to artists from Muddy Waters to Eric Clapton, and it also holds an extensive collection of both guitars and harmonicas. The cutting-edge interactive technology makes this a museum worth visiting. Also connected to the museum is Bluesville, a 1,000-seat complex where live acts perform year-round. (800) 303-7463.

Bellisimo Spa. Grand Casino Tunica, 13615 Old Highway 61 North, Robinsonville, MS 38664. Rolling the dice and bending over game tables can really take a toll on your body. So when you're ready to relax, slip into Bellisimo Spa for the pampering of a lifetime. This full-service spa offers treatments for your hands, feet, face, and entire body. For a full listing of spa packages, visit www.grandtunica.com or call (800) WIN-4WIN.

River Bend Links Golf Course. 1205 Nine Links Drive, Robinsonville, MS 38664. This 6,900-yard plan offers the most discriminating golfer a game worth remembering. There are five courses to choose from, all designed by Clyde Johnston. www.riverbendlinks.com. (888) 539-9990.

CASINOS

Gold Strike Casino. 1010 Casino Center Drive, Robinsonville, MS 38664. Fittingly, the Gold Strike Casino stands out because of its golden facade. The hotel inside the casino boasts oversized rooms, while the casino itself is an amazing combination of brass, wood, and marble. www.goldstrike.com. (800) 245-7829.

Grand Casino Tunica. 13615 Old Highway 61 North, Robinsonville, MS 38664. By far the largest resort in Tunica, this gaming center has earned its name. The Grand Casino features 110 table games, 3,100 slot machines, a 200-space RV park, three hotels, nine restaurants, and Willows Sporting Clays. You could literally lose yourself at the Grand Casino Tunica. www.tunicamiss.org. (800) WIN-4WIN.

Sam's Town. 1477 Casino Center Drive, Robinsonville, MS 38664. Sam's Town claims the "hottest" slots and table games within the casino, and luxurious suites in its hotel. Along with more than 30,000 square feet of meeting, banquet, and exhibit space, Sam's Town also houses the extraordinary Emporium—a shopper's paradise. www.samstown.com. (800) 456-0711.

Bally's Saloon, Gambling Hall & Hotel. 1450 Bally's Boulevard, Robinsonville, MS 38664. Get a feel for the Old West at Bally's. The contrasting wood and velvet in this casino's interior enrich the feel of days gone by. Bally's features a selection of restaurants, including the Delta Levee Cafe. You'll find 40,000 square feet of gaming space, a 235-room hotel, an exercise room, and a pool. Best of all, Bally's is home to the Silo Club, a 250-seat nightclub built into an actual grain silo. www.ballysms.com. (800) 38-BALLY (382-2559).

Fitzgerald's Casino. 711 Lucky Lane, Robinsonville, MS 38664. Fitzgerald's is the only casino in Tunica actually located on the banks of the Mississippi River, providing for some spectacular views of the river and its traffic. The casino is built with an Irish castle theme, which includes a chance to touch a piece of the authentic Blarney Stone for good luck. (800) 766-LUCK (5825).

WHERE TO SHOP

On a Whim. 985 Magnolia, Tunica, MS 38676. This gift shop has it all. From baby items to gourmet foods, the selections are limitless. On a Whim also features Mississippi-made products and specialty gift baskets. (662) 363-3336.

Casino Factory Shoppes. 1000 Highway 61, Tunica, MS 38676. Twenty retail outlet stores and counting, the Casino Factory Shoppes have an abundance of places to stop and shop. Choose from CHAPS Ralph Lauren, Linen Barn Factory Outlet, Rue 21, L'eggs Hanes Bali Playtex, and Carter's Childrenswear to name a few. (662) 363-2200.

WHERE TO EAT

Café Marie. 6195 Fox Island Road, Tunica, MS 38676. In addition to delicate offerings of beef, pork, or fowl seasoned with unique Dixie spices, this cafe also has a real old-fashioned soda fountain. $-$$; ☐. (662) 357-0055.

Blue and White Restaurant. 1355 US 61 North, Tunica, MS 38676. One of Mississippi's most famous restaurants, the Blue and White has been a resting point for many a traveler in the South. Since its opening in the early 1940s, this dining establishment has been serving southern-style home cooking in buffet style. You won't want to leave town without trying the fresh, home-cooked vegetables served daily. Offerings generally include fried chicken, rice and gravy, and peas, to name a few. $-$$; ☐. (662) 363-1371.

The Hollywood Café. 1130 Old Commerce Road, Tunica, MS 38676. If you've heard the song "Walking in Memphis," you've heard about the Hollywood. But did you know how it came to be? It was started by a college student who was home during summer break. He felt there was a need for a simple but good food joint in the area, and when it came time for him to head back to school at the end of the summer, the locals had acquired such a taste for his food, they decided to keep it open. Originally the Hollywood was built in the community of Hollywood, Mississippi, and remained there until it burned in the late 1970s. The Hollywood is known for miles around as being the "Home of the Fried Dill Pickle." But come hungry, because this world-famous dive also makes a mean fried catfish. $-$$; ☐. (662) 363-1126.

Limericks Steakhouse. 711 Lucky Lane, Robinsonville, MS 38664. Named by the *Washington Post* as "the best of casino restaurants in Tunica," Limericks offers a wide variety of items—from steaks, seafood, and game to gourmet salads and outrageous desserts. $$-$$$; ☐. (800) 766-LUCK.

Cafe Sonoma. 1021 Casino Center Drive, Robinsonville, MS 38664. Considered by many a Memphian the finest dining establishment in Tunica, Cafe Sonoma offers patrons an elaborate selection. Some of the menu favorites include the lobster cake appetizers, seafood sampler, and lamb. And save room for dessert—the crème brûlée and tiramisu are to die for. Are you hungry yet? $$-$$$; ☐. (800) 303-7463.

WHERE TO STAY

The Cottage Inn. 4325 Casino Center Drive, Robinsonville, MS 38664. The Cottage Inn is comprised of ten luxury chalets, each with two individual guest rooms. Each room includes a refrigerator, microwave, and coffeemaker; a gazebo with fireplace, wet bar, and grill is available to all guests, making this a romantic getaway in the midst of the Mississippi Delta. There is a complimentary continental breakfast, and pets are allowed. $$-$$$; ☐. www.cottageinn-chalet.com. (800) 363-2985.

Levee Plantation Guest House. Plantation Road, Robinsonville, MS 38664. The Levee Plantation Guest House is the height of luxury, offering a quiet, scenic atmosphere just minutes away from the gaming action of Tunica. The Guest House has a bedroom, living room, kitchen area, screened porch, two baths, covered parking, and a flower garden. Best of all, service is customized to meet your individual needs. $$$; ☐. (662) 363-1309.

SPECIAL EVENTS

Tunica Rivergate Festival. April. This fun festival is also a sanctioned Memphis in May event. Festivities include a barbecue cooking contest, children's games and activities, a petting zoo, rides, food, and live entertainment. Best of all—admission is totally free. (662) 363-2865.

Tunica Harvest Festival. October. The staple in this area is agriculture, so the Harvest Festival gives locals and visitors a chance to celebrate it. The festival includes a display of farm implements, produce, and local crops, as well as an assembly of artisans who reflect the days gone by. Among the festival events are a chili cook-off and a 5K run. (662) 363-2865.

MERIGOLD

From Tunica, continue down US 61 south to Merigold, home of the renowned Mississippi artists and potters Lee and Pup McCarty. Visitors can tour the grounds and gallery of the McCartys by wandering through a bamboo tunnel and into an elaborate garden, filled with rare herbs and indigenous plants and trees. The artists' studio itself is built from the remains of an old mule barn.

McCarty Pottery Barn and Gallery Restaurant. 101 South Saint Mary Street, Merigold, MS 38759. Visit the spot where the McCartys create their world-famous pottery from Mississippi River mud. And stop in the Gallery for a quick bit to eat at lunchtime. The menu features an interesting and ever-changing selection of dishes, all served on dinnerware made by the McCartys themselves. (662) 748-2293.

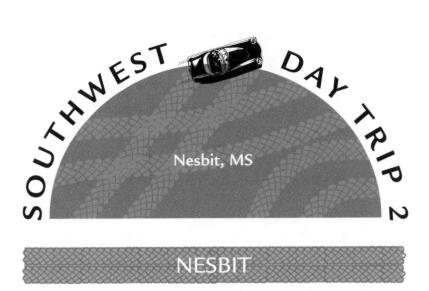

NESBIT

From Memphis, take I-55 into Mississippi. Just a few miles from the state line, turn off onto the Church Road exit, and follow the winding road to the secluded Bonne Terre Inn. Once you arrive, you'll feel like you're a million miles away from the big city. And Bonne Terre is what Nesbit is all about. So park your car, enter the estate, and settle in for the day—or the weekend.

WHERE TO GO

Bonne Terre Country Inn and Cafe. 4715 Church Road West, Nesbit, MS 38651. Bonne Terre means "good earth," and it was a dream-come-true for innkeeper Max Bonnin and his late wife, June. Once you sleep on one of Bonne Terre's incredible feather beds, you'll never want to leave this haven of serenity. Choose from fifteen majestic rooms, all of which can be seen on Bonne Terre's Web site. Each has been carefully decorated with fine art and French and English antiques collected by Max and June Bonnin over the years. The inn also has a pool, Jacuzzi tubs, three lakes, and a trail that meanders through an astonishing panorama of wildflowers. Over the years, it has become the location of choice for many a Southern wedding. Activities include fly fishing and hayrides.

In the cafe Chef Antony Field creates sumptuous seasonal offerings and specialty menus that make Bonne Terre worth the drive. For parties of six or more, a complimentary limousine ride can be

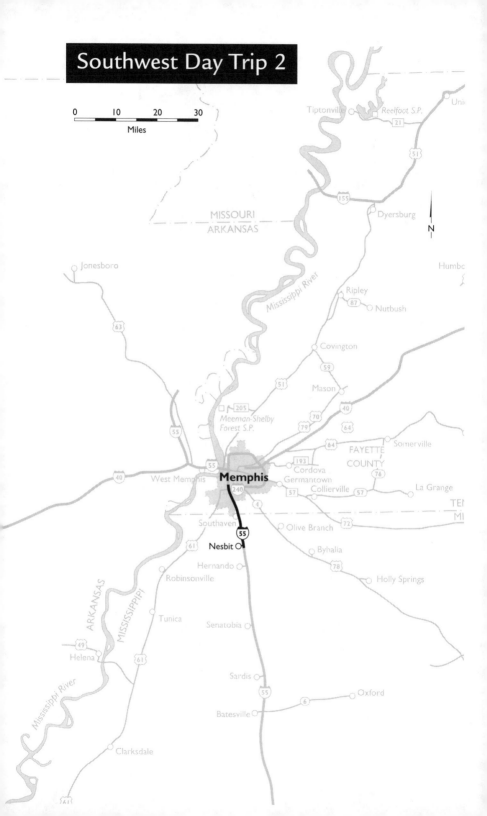

Southwest Day Trip 2

0   10   20   30
Miles

arranged through the cafe. Many Memphians visit Bonne Terre just for the meals, and with selections like white chocolate soup, Louisiana veal scaloppine and apple-brandy-glazed shrimp, who can blame them? Open for dinner Tuesday through Saturday, the cafe also offers a jazz brunch once a month, as well as lunch every Tuesday and Thursday. But call before you come, because you want a table waiting at the end of this delectable journey.

If you're looking for a unique gift, then head over to Bonne Gifts—it's located across from the cafe. This specialty shop carries a full line of bath products, pewter and silver gifts, pottery, and delightful finds for children, as well as Bonne Terre logo merchandise. $$$; ☐. www.bonneterre.com. (662) 781-5199.

Fogg Road Herb Farm. 706 Fogg Road, Nesbit, MS 38651. Fogg Road Herb Farm is the home of "Cooking 'n Crafting with Herbs" instructional classes. It boasts more than forty varieties of herbs, edible flowers, peppers, leeks, tomatoes, and the like. You can purchase both herbs and plants at this delightful farm, open April through June, Tuesday through Saturday. (662) 429-4959.

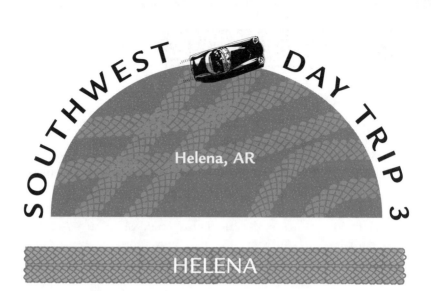

Helena, AR

SOUTHWEST DAY TRIP 3

HELENA

Ironically, the easiest way to get to Helena, Arkansas, is via Mississippi. From Memphis hop on I-55 until you see the exit for US 61 south (exit 7), which takes you toward Vicksburg. US 61 changes names a few times but eventually rights itself. Don't panic if you suddenly look up and see that you're on South Third Street or TN 14. After 45 or so miles, turn right onto US 49 west, cross the Mississippi River, and say hello to Arkansas, former home of President Clinton. Helena is just another 11 miles farther west. The final distance tally will be right around 70 miles.

Once you arrive, you'll get to experience life in the Arkansas Delta and bayous, famous for delta blues among music lovers. The well-maintained Delta Cultural Center is the perfect place to start your day: You'll learn both the history of Helena and its surrounding area as well as the story of the delta blues. Then make your way through the town's charming historic district located at Holly, College, and Perry Streets and tour the Pillow-Thompson House. Before you leave town, be sure to make a stop at the Helena Murals, which chronicle even more of the blues.

WHERE TO GO

Helena Chamber of Commerce. 111 Hickory Hills Drive, Helena, AR 72342. Helena's chamber of commerce will provide you with maps and information about the area, including West Helena. (870) 838-8327.

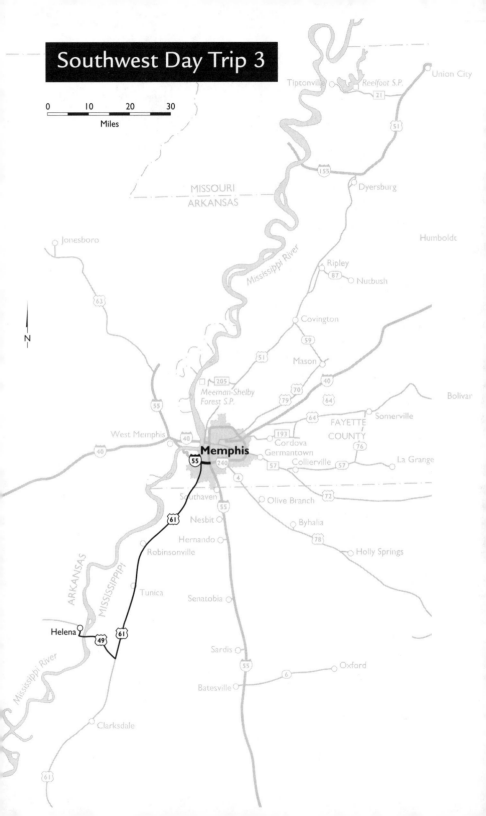

Southwest Day Trip 3

0   10   20   30
Miles

Tiptonville   Reelfoot S.P.   Union City
21

51

155

Dyersburg

MISSOURI
ARKANSAS

Humboldt

Jonesboro

Ripley   Nutbush
87

Mississippi River

Covington

59

63

Mason

51   70   40
64

Bolivar

205

Meeman-Shelby
Forest S.P.

79

64   FAYETTE
COUNTY   Somerville

55

West Memphis   193
Cordova   76

40   Memphis   Germantown
55   240   Collierville   57   La Grange
57

4

Southaven
55

72

Olive Branch

61   Nesbit   Byhalia

Hernando   78

Robinsonville   Holly Springs

ARKANSAS   MISSISSIPPI

Tunica   Senatobia

Helena
49   61

Sardis
55

6   Oxford

Mississippi River   Batesville

Clarksdale

61

Delta Cultural Center. 141 Cherry Street, Helena, AR 72342. For more than a decade, visitors have gone to the Delta Cultural Center to learn the history and culture of the Arkansas Delta, its people, and its prosperous land. It's the absolute must-see in Helena. The DCC is actually housed in three separate locations, with the two main buildings only a block apart. The visitor center is the central location and houses a museum store, a gallery for temporary exhibits, and a permanent music-of-the-delta exhibit, which includes listening stations and video showings of the King Biscuit Blues Festival.

Just a block away at 95 Missouri Street, you'll find the depot, a restored 1912 train station, which maintains the permanent collection of Arkansas Delta heritage. Themes of the exhibit include the Civil War, Native American life, African American culture, and Old Man River. This last exhibit has particular interest for Memphians because in its depiction of the story of rivers, it focuses on the life and times of the Mississippi: who controlled it, when it flooded (especially in 1927), and how steamboats traveled on it.

Finally, the Moore-Hornor House, located at 323 Beech Street, is a mid-nineteenth-century Greek Revival home on the National Register of Historic Places. Its backyard was the site of some bloody fighting in the battle of Helena in 1863. www.deltaculturalcenter.com. (800) 358-0972 .

Helena Murals. 100 Cherry Street, Helena, AR 72342. After learning the heritage of the delta at the Cultural Center, head up the street to the Helena Murals. The seawall roadside painting tells the story of the blues and of Helena's early days. You'll also find a mural located at US 49B, just as you cross Crowley's Ridge going into West Helena.

Pillow-Thompson House. 718 Perry Street, Helena, AR 72342. This pristine example of southern Queen Anne architecture was built in 1896 by Jerome Pillow and designed by George Barber, a popular Helena architect of the late nineteenth century. The house was recently restored to its early grandeur. Five generations of the Pillow family have lived here. Visitors can tour the authentically furnished home and on Tuesday join in the weekly luncheon (reservations are needed for lunch). Paula Oliver, who owns Oliver's restaurant, is the director of the PT House and can answer any of your questions about the building and most of your questions about Helena. Occasionally, like on Valentine's Day, the Pillow-Thompson

House hosts special dinners. If you're interested in planning your day trip around such an event, call ahead to find out when the next one will be. Free. Open Tuesday through Sunday, except major holidays. (870) 338–8535.

Confederate Military Cemetery. If you're a Civil War buff, you'll want to check out the Confederate Military Cemetery. Among the hundred graves, you may find a soldier's name you know. From the cemetery, you'll also have a grand view of the Mississippi River. To get there, just head down Cherry Street toward the statue and keep going. The cemetery doesn't have an exact address, but it's located on Holly Street.

WHERE TO SHOP

Bubba's Blues Corner. 105 Cherry Street, Helena, AR 73242. If all that delta blues history has you hankering for some music of your own, stop in at Bubba's and browse through the vast collection of blues LPs, CDs, tapes, books, and memorabilia. There's an amazing number of blues-lovers' artifacts here, and the owner says that several Memphians make the trip frequently just to dig through the bins for anything new. ☐. (870) 338–3501.

WHERE TO EAT

Oliver's. 101 Missouri Street, Helena, AR 72342. According to the locals, there's really only one place to eat nowadays—Oliver's. Jerry and Paula Oliver opened their restaurant in the fall of 2000, and it's been a great success. Located at the end of Cherry Street, just next door to the Delta Cultural Center's depot, Oliver's is easy to get to. Lunch is served cafe-style: a variety of sandwiches, soups, and salads, and a "plate" special of one meat and three vegetables. When the sun sets, Oliver's dims the lights to create a full dinner restaurant, serving "inch-thick" steaks and a wide selection of chicken, seafood, and pasta dishes. $-$$; ☐. (870) 338–7228.

WHERE TO STAY

Edwardian Inn. 317 Biscoe, Helena, AR 72342-3630. Built in 1905, the Edwardian is an absolutely magnificent example of Colonial Revival, and you'll catch your breath as you approach this grand mansion on the hill. All twelve of the rooms are named for famous Helena natives and can best be described as "premium": They offer all the amenities, including private bath and privately controlled air-conditioning and heating. The interior of the house itself has exceptional woodwork with quarter-sawn oak paneling and nine original mantels. On the first floor, pay attention to the "wood carpeting," which is German-made and consists of thirty-six types of wood. Guests are served a hearty breakfast, compliments of John Crow, the owner. And if you phone ahead, John can arrange a discounted rate for a weekend package. The Edwardian is listed on the National Register of Historic Places. $$; ☐. (870) 338-9155.

Magnolia Hill. 608 Perry Street, Helena, AR 72342. If you're looking for some history in your accommodations, settle into the Magnolia Hill bed-and-breakfast. Though it's only ten minutes from the Mississippi casinos, you'll feel like you've gone to another world. Magnolia Hill is a Queen Anne home, built in 1895, and listed on the National Register of Historic Places. James and Jane Insco have created a cozy but elegant enclave of eight guest rooms, all with private bath and antique furnishings. In addition to the historic atmosphere and fabulous porch, you'll enjoy cable television and complimentary chocolate, fruit, and beverages, not to mention the gourmet breakfast that's served in the dining room. $$; ☐. (870) 338-6874.

Foxglove Bed & Breakfast. 229 Beech, Helena, AR 72342. Like Magnolia Hill, Foxglove was built more than a hundred years ago—1900, to be exact—and is a National Register property. Consistent with its Victorian style, the front porch beckons travelers to sit and enjoy the view. It's only 65 miles from Memphis, five minutes from both the Mississippi casinos and Helena's downtown shops, and situated on Crowley's Ridge, which overlooks historic Helena and the Mississippi River. This is a luxury inn, offering seven guest rooms, all with private bath (and some with whirlpool tubs), along with antiques, parquet floors, stained glass, and numerous turn-of-the-twentieth century fireplaces. You'll be on a first-name basis with the owners, John and Jessie, as they serve up their specialty in the morning: Christmas Eggs. $$; ☐. (800) 863-1926.

Stone Ridge Inn. 1202 Perry Street, Helena, AR 73242. Stone Ridge, like the other bed-and-breakfasts listed here, is a National Register property. It consists of two homes—the Cassidy and the

Altman—located in the historic district of Helena, just a few minutes from the antiques shops, Delta Cultural Center, and Riverfront Park. Both offer a variety of elegantly furnished rooms and suites, some with fireplaces, sitting rooms, and minikitchens. For photographs of every room, check out the Web site, www.stoneridgeinns.com. $$; ☐. (870) 338-9390.

SPECIAL EVENTS

Wild Hog Music Festival and Motocycle Rally. April. Wild Hog is both a music festival with live performances throughout the weekend and a bikers' rally with a Harley Davidson giveaway. (870) 338-8327.

   King Biscuit Blues Festival. October. Otherwise known as the Delta's Premier Blues Festival, the "Biscuit" has been around since the mid-1980s, when it began as a celebration of Helena's blues roots and of famous blues musician Sonny Boy Williamson. Today the festival runs for four days, with musicians performing on five stages. www.kingbiscuitfest.org. (870) 338-8798.

DOWNTOWN MEMPHIS

It may seem a bit extravagant to make a day trip out of heading to the westernmost point of your own city, but the revitalization of downtown keeps locals and visitors coming back for more. Union and Poplar both feed city traffic into the heart of downtown. But however you get here, you'll be glad you came. With all of the renovation that's been going on downtown, if you haven't visited the heart of the city lately, you may not even recognize it. Founded in 1819, Memphis is currently the eighteenth largest city in the nation. The downtown area is laid out in a grid, consistent to our founding fathers' scale of the city. This city on the river, named for its Egyptian counterpart on the Nile, has lots to be proud of. From blues to barbecue, Memphis has made a national name for itself here on the banks of the Mighty Mississippi.

WHERE TO GO

Memphis Convention and Visitors Bureau. 47 Union Avenue, Memphis, TN 38103. Before you take a trek around downtown, stop by the Convention and Visitors Bureau to pick up some great brochures about the city. And don't leave without getting a copy of the special addition of the *Official Visitors Guide to Memphis*—it's jammed full of activities all around town. (901) 543-5300.

   Trolley Tour. 547 North Main Street, Memphis, TN 38103. One of the easiest ways to get a tour of downtown Memphis is by way of the trolleys. The line runs from South Main down to the riverfront, and stops frequently along the way. All of Memphis's trolleys are antique and have been bought from cities around the United States. Attraction stops along the way include the Pyramid, Pinch District, Memphis Cook Convention Center, Beale Street, Orpheum Theatre, and the National Civil Rights Museum. (901) 274-6282.

Beale Street Historic District. 203 Beale Street, Memphis, TN 38103. If Memphis is home of the blues, then this is where it was conceived. Musicians such as W. C. Handy took crowds by storm and put Memphis on the map with their unique style of music. Since then, this has become one of the most famous streets in America. Wander down the street and duck into any of the bars to catch a

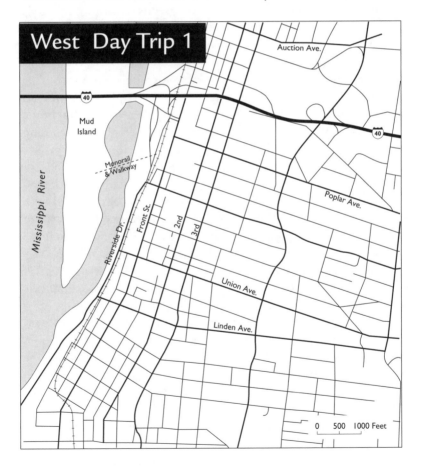

local up-and-coming star or to hear the tunes of times gone by. www.bealestreet.com. (901) 526-0125.

Center for Southern Folklore. 119 South Main Street, Memphis, TN 38103. The traditions of the South come alive here at the center where visitors can look through folk art, crafts, and photography exhibits. Sit a spell in the cafe and listen to live music, including blues, country, soul, rockabilly, and gospel. Open daily. (901) 525-3655.

Fire Museum of Memphis. 118 Adams Avenue, Memphis, TN 38103. This has become a popular spot for children's birthday parties, and no wonder. What a wonderful way to combine fire safety and fun through a museum! The museum includes an elaborate collection of artifacts, stories, and photographs of some of the city's most devastating fires. The museum also is home to an animated "talking" horse. And children are drawn to the interactive games that teach fire safety. (901) 320-5650.

Magevney House. 198 Adams Avenue, Memphis, TN 38103. This historic home was built in the mid-1830s and was home to Memphis's first schoolteacher, Eugene Magevney. The home remains as it was during the period in which it was built, including original furnishings and decor. (901) 526-4464.

Memphis Rock 'n' Soul Museum. 145 Lieutenant George W. Lee Avenue, Memphis, TN 38103. This incredible museum is part of the Smithsonian Institution, and offers a look at the birth and growth of blues, soul, and rock and roll over the past century. Connected to the museum is the Gibson Guitar Plant, where you can watch the progression of the instrument in the making. (901) 543-0800.

Mud Island River Park. 125 North Front Street, Memphis, TN 38103. The trip to this park begins with an exciting monorail ride over the Mississippi River. Once you land on the island, you can tour the Mississippi River Museum, which contains more than a dozen galleries dedicated to the history and preservation of the river. A favorite spot at the park is the River Walk, a to-scale replica of the entire Mississippi River. (901) 576-7241.

National Civil Rights Museum. 450 Mulberry Street, Memphis, TN 38013. On April 4, 1968, Martin Luther King Jr. was assassinated at the Lorraine Motel. Today that motel has been transformed into a museum commemorating the strikes and protests during the civil rights movement. As you enter the gates, don't be alarmed to see a woman positioned across the street in protest. She's been a part of the scenery for more than a decade, picketing to protest her removal from the motel where she'd lived so it could be made into a national museum. In addition to the permanent exhibit, the National Civil Rights Museum hosts a variety of other exhibits year-round. Open Monday, Wednesday, and Saturday. www.civilrightsmuseum.org. (901) 521-9699.

National Ornamental Metal Museum. 374 Metal Museum Drive, Memphis, TN 38106. This is the only institution in the entire country dedicated entirely to the collection and exhibition of metalwork. It's open Tuesday through Sunday, and exhibits rotate regularly. (901) 774-6380.

Peabody Place Museum. 119 South Main Street, Memphis, TN 38103. This exhibition hall is dedicated to the incredible artwork of China. Tourists can see more than 400 art pieces, including a cinnabar red lacquer chair inlaid with dragons, made for a Chinese emperor. Admission is charged, and the museum is closed Monday. (901) 523-ARTS.

Slavehaven/Burkle Estate Museum. 826 North Second Street, Memphis, TN 38107. This museum was once a way station on the Underground Railroad, the slaves' road to freedom. Explore the secret cellars, trapdoors, and escape route taken by runaway slaves. The museum is covered with a collection of old advertisements and other artifacts. Closed Tuesday and Wednesday. (901) 527-3427.

Sun Studio. 706 Union Avenue, Memphis, TN 38103. It was on this record label that stars like Elvis Presley, B. B. King, Johnny Cash, Jerry Lee Lewis, Howlin' Wolf, and Roy Orbison came into the spotlight. Considered the birthplace of rock and roll, Sun Studios is a must-see for any downtown visitor. There is an admission fee for anyone over twelve years old. Tours are conducted from 10:00 A.M. until 5:30 P.M. www.sunstudio.com. (901) 521-0664.

Viking Culinary Arts Center. 119 South Main Street, #600, Memphis, TN 38103. This is no ordinary kitchen store—it's an experience. The center combines a world-class teaching kitchen with state-of-the-art theater demonstrations for those who attend the multitude of cooking classes. Of course, if you don't have time to actually cook, you won't want to miss the incredible shop that offers any chef some of the handiest professional-grade tools on the market. (901) 578-5822.

Woodruff-Fontaine House. 680 Adams Avenue, Memphis, TN 38111. This breathtaking mansion built in 1870 has been fully restored to capture the feel of the original French Victorian home. All three stories have been furnished with Victorian furniture and accessories, and the home contains a large collection of period clothing. During the holidays, volunteers transform the home into a picturesque presentation of Christmas from long ago. Each room is decorated in holiday trimming, and the dining room is set for a Christmas meal. (901) 526-1469.

AutoZone Park. 8 South Third Street, Memphis, TN 38103. This incredible stadium is the best of its kind. Home to the Cardinals' AAA affiliate, the Memphis Redbirds, AutoZone Park is awesome to tour even if there's not a game. Of course, you won't want to miss out on the Redbirds, the only not-for-profit team in the nation. Located in the heart of downtown, the ballpark features "Nostalgia Man" and the Backstop Emporium. For games and ticket information, call (901) 721-6000.

The Pyramid. 1 Auction Avenue, Memphis, TN 38103. It's only fitting that a city named for a city in Egypt have its own pyramid. But this pyramid is no burial ground—unless you happen to be playing the University of Memphis Tigers, in which case the Pyramid quickly acquires a new name, the "Tomb of Doom." Otherwise, this thirty-two-story, 21,000-seat sports arena hosts a variety of national tournaments, entertainment, and family shows. Check the Web site for schedules and performances: www.pyramidarena.com. (901) 521-9675.

See Memphis. 378 South Main Street, Memphis, TN 38103. Whether you're planning a trip for out-of-town visitors or just want to become better acquainted with our city, See Memphis tours can show you all the sights. Group and individual tours available. (901) 525-4617.

Carriage Tours of Memphis. 393 North Main, Memphis, TN 38103. What could be more romantic than riding in a horse-drawn carriage? Experience this magic while touring some of the most popular sites in downtown Memphis, and get an intriguing story of this great city from your carriage driver. (901) 527-7542.

WHERE TO SHOP

The Charcoal Store and Pert's Patio. 136 G. E. Patterson Avenue, Memphis, TN 38103. The Charcoal Store has lots of unique gifts for the home and patio. There's also an elaborate collection of metalwork, as well as a large selection of chimeneas, flowerpots, baker's racks, and decorative archways. (901) 578-8086.

Carabella's. 85 Second Street, Memphis, TN 38103. Offering gifts and selections for the home or garden, Carabella's is one of the most unusual shops in downtown Memphis. The children's area has a number of specialty items, and don't miss the fun array of cocktail napkins for sale. It's also easy to find—right across the street from the landmark Peabody Hotel. (901) 525-5500.

Carnavale. 530 South Main Street, Memphis, TN 38103. Owned and operated by Memphian John Simmons, Carnavale has tons of fun and funky accessories for the home. Along the back wall is an incredible selection of place mats, Simmons's signature creation. These mats are made locally and come in every shade imaginable. (901) 544-7044.

The Corkscrew. 511 South Front Street, Memphis, TN 38103. This wine shop is the best of the best—it boasts the finest selection of wines downtown. Featuring a wide array of imports, domestics, champagne and spirits, the Corkscrew has made a great addition to downtown Memphis. Check out the Web site for specials and discounts: www.thecorkscrew.com. (901) 543-9463.

The Nile Egyptian Museum Gift Shop. 548 South Main Street, Memphis, TN 38103. Of course Memphis has a store dedicated to everything Egyptian, and this is it. Pick up some interesting artwork or collectibles. (901) 523-8151.

Y-Not. 333 Beale Street, Memphis, TN 38103. Let's face it—if you've traveled all the way to Beale Street, chances are you need some kitschy memorabilia to take home with you. And that's just what you'll find at Y-Not: anything from Elvis license plates and driver's licenses to touristy T-shirts. Y-Not claims to be "the ultimate in Beale Street souvenirs." (901) 527-9084.

ICB's Outlet Store. 137 G. E. Patterson Avenue, Memphis, TN 38103. *ICB* stands for "I see bargains," and that statement is correct indeed. Inside this outlet store, find name-brand furnishings and accessories that have been marked down tremendously. The rooms are divided into types—some for slipcovers and window treatments, some for fabric, and others for rugs. (901) 529-1576.

Perez Cigar Company. 87 South Main Street, Memphis, TN 38103. The Cigar Company has become a mainstay on the trolley line tour, with locals and tourists alike stopping in for premium hand-rolled cigars. It also offers smoking accessories, gifts, and gourmet teas and coffees. Occasionally, there's live music in front of the store. And there is, of course, a cigar-store Indian to greet patrons by the door. www.perezcompany.com. (901) 521-6111.

WHERE TO EAT

Blues City Cafe. 138 Beale Street, Memphis, TN 38103. This rib joint is a favorite around town and nationwide. When President Clinton visited Memphis, he dined in this spot, known for its late-night service. The Blues City Cafe also offers a mean hot tamale. Patrons can enjoy live music nightly in the Bandbox, and can take home souvenirs from the Blues City General Store. $$; □. (901) 526-3637.

   The Arcade. 540 South Main Street, Memphis, TN 38103. The Arcade is the oldest cafe in town. Located across from Central Station, it has served many a meal to those just passing through on the train. Of course, its incredible menu kept it open even when the train stopped running. Today diners can enjoy grits and beignets at breakfast or hearty slices of homemade pizza at lunch. $$; □. (901) 526-5757.

   The Butcher Shop. 101 South Front Street, Memphis, TN 38103. At the Butcher Shop, you can cook your own steaks over a hickory charcoal grill, or select the marinated chicken or salmon from the menu. Whatever you do, plan plenty of time for this stop, because an experience at the Butcher Shop is one you'll want to savor. $$$; □. (901) 521-0856.

   Cafe Samovar. 83 Union Avenue, Memphis, TN 38103. The sign out front reads FROM RUSSIA WITH LUNCH, and Cafe Samovar has indeed become one of the most popular lunch spots for many downtown employees. This little cafe offers Memphians big taste when it comes to Eastern European cuisine. Try the daily soup of the chef's choice, or the Russian Bellini—crepes filled with chicken and a hearty sauce. Dinner is more upscale, with selections changing regularly. Cafe Samovar also offers the largest selection of vodkas in Memphis, and live entertainment in the form of belly dancers on Friday and Saturday nights. Open Monday through Friday for lunch; Monday through Saturday for dinner. $$-$$$; □. (901) 529-9607.

Chez Philippe. 149 Union Avenue, Memphis, TN 38103. Chez Philippe is the most luxurious restaurant downtown has to offer. The ornate dining room is a replica of French grandeur, and the menu matches the atmosphere. Select from items such as game meats and seafoods prepared by Jose Gutierrez, one of the nation's most renowned chefs. Make reservations in advance; a coat is required for gentlemen. Open only for dinner Monday through Saturday. $$$; ☐. (901) 529-9607.

Dyer's. 205 Beale Street, Memphis, TN 38103. Known throughout the Midsouth for one of the most unusual dishes of its kind—a deep-fried burger. While there are other items on the menu, who could resist one of these mouthwatering, sinfully delicious treats? $-$$; ☐. (901) 527-3937.

Elvis Presley's Memphis. 126 Beale Street, Memphis, TN 38103. Elvis is remembered as saying, "Someone once asked me what I missed most about Memphis. I told them 'everything.' " And that's just what this restaurant is—a tribute to everything Elvis. From stage costumes to sideburns, Elvis Presley's Memphis captures it all. And the menu reflects some of Elvis's favorite meals, including meat loaf and a fried peanut butter and banana sandwich. On Sunday patrons can enjoy the Gospel Brunch as a choir serenades them. Open daily. $$; ☐. (901) 527-6900.

Cielo. 679 Adams Avenue, Memphis, TN 38103. Just as the name implies, this restaurant is truly heavenly. It is the creation of Karen Blockman-Carrier, who has been featured on the Food Network. Cielo is located inside the historical Molly Fontaine Home in the heart of Memphis's Victorian Village. The menu reflects influences from South America, the Caribbean, and the Pacific Rim. Upstairs is a cozy bar area where patrons can gather around the piano and enjoy an evening cocktail. The atmosphere inside this charming restaurant matches the menu—eclectic and elegant. Open for dinner Tuesday through Saturday; lunch is served Tuesday through Friday. $$$; ☐. (901) 524-1886.

The Little Tea Shop. 69 Monroe Avenue, Memphis, TN 38103. The Little Tea Shop boasts of being "downtown's lunch place since 1918," and it doesn't disappoint. Hearty servings of vegetables and entrees change daily, but one of the menu's staples is the Lacy Special—a chicken breast smothered in gravy and placed atop buttered corn sticks. And save room for dessert, because the homemade cobbler is a tempting end to any meal. Open for lunch only. $$. (901) 525-6000.

The Rendezvous. 52 South Second Street, Memphis, TN 38103. The Rendezvous has been a Memphis tradition since 1948. Today people order its world-famous ribs to be shipped overnight. Some of the more popular items on the menu include a full slab of ribs, the cheese and sausage platter, and the barbecued pork loin. Located in a basement along a downtown alley, the Rendezvous is a popular spot for celebrities and locals alike. $$; ☐. 523-2746.

Automatic Slim's Tonga Club. 83 South Second Street Memphis, TN 38103. Slim's menu is seasoned with southwestern- and Caribbean-inspired dishes. Items such as jerk chicken and duck quesadillas are popular lunch selections. The dinner menu features rotating specials, but many patrons stop by to see and be seen at the Tonga Club bar. Automatic Slim's, with its animal-print seats and funky lighting, is a popular spot indeed. Live bands perform on the weekends. $$-$$$; ☐. (901) 525-7948.

WHERE TO STAY

The Peabody Hotel. 149 Union Avenue, Memphis, TN 38103. It's called the South's Grand Hotel, and the Peabody is just that. Inside, you'll find 468 luxurious rooms, four award-winning restaurants, unique gift shops, and an athletic club with indoor pool. The Peabody is a downtown icon, mostly because of the Marching Ducks, a fleet of ducks trained to walk the red carpet each morning to the center of the lobby, where they spend the day wading leisurely in the enormous marble fountain. The Peabody is a perfect selection for a romantic weekend getaway, and is within walking distance of most downtown attractions. $$$; ☐. (901) 529-4000.

Talbot Heirs Guesthouse. 99 South Second Street, Memphis, TN 38103. Quietly nestled beside an array of downtown buildings is the Talbot Heirs Guesthouse. This uncommon alternative to a hotel has served as a resting spot for many a famous visitor wishing to escape the limelight yet remain completely pampered. There are four spaces to choose from, each with unique decor. All come with the comforts of home. Select a room by viewing pictures on the Web site. $$$; ☐. www.talbothouse.com. (901) 527-9772.

MISSISSIPPI RIVER

If you've already reached downtown Memphis, then head to Riverside Drive. As you follow the banks of the Mississippi River, you'll see a large area of cobblestones. These cobblestones have a remarkable history—they've withstood both battles and yellow fever, and continue to welcome visitors to the Mighty Mississippi. From 1811 to the turn of the twentieth century, the paddlewheel steamboat grew in popularity throughout America; at one time thousands of these boats moved about our nation's waterways and were major contributors to development. Everything from cattle to imported fabrics could be moved across the country with ease. And as American economy boomed, cities like Memphis came to be developed along the water's edge.

Although long since replaced by the railroad, autos, and airplanes, given all today's hustle and bustle there's still something magical about stepping aboard a steamboat and waltzing around the deck. It's as if Mark Twain might appear at any moment. But even if he doesn't, there is plenty to keep you entertained on these modern-day boats. Cruises last anywhere from two hours to twelve days—take your pick!

WHERE TO GO

Memphis Queen **Line Riverboat.** 45 Riverside Drive, Memphis, TN 38103. From March through November, the *Memphis Queen* is the

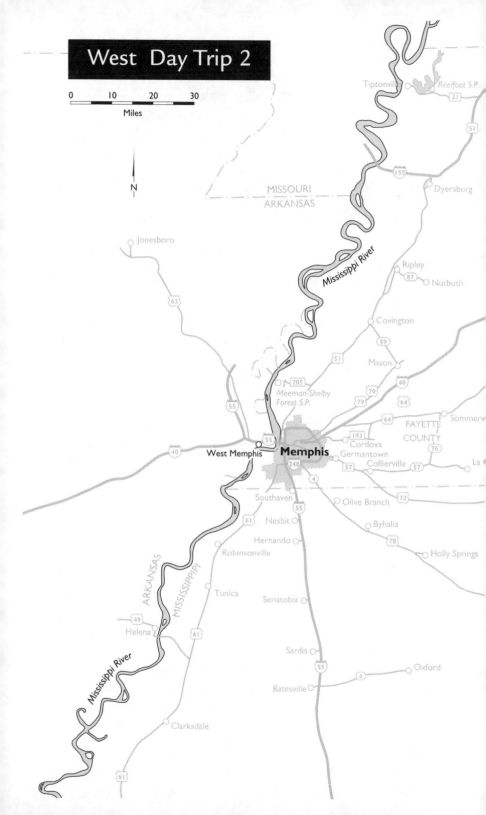

best way to get a sight-seeing tour of the Mississippi River around Memphis. The riverboat travels 5 miles south down the Mississippi side of the river, returning up the Arkansas side. You can take a sight-seeing tour for $12.50 for adults, $11.50 for seniors, and $9.50 for children. If you opt for the more romantic dinner cruise, prices range from $31.95 for adults and $24.95 for children. (901) 527-5694.

Delta Queen Tours. Robin Street Wharf, New Orleans, LA 70114. Even though the company is based in New Orleans, Delta Queen Tours pick up sightseers from the banks of the Mississippi in downtown Memphis. Depending on the time of year, Delta Queen Tours offers incredible vacations up and down the Mighty Mississippi on one of three steamboats—the *Delta Queen,* the *Mississippi Queen,* or the *American Queen.* Every cruise includes four meals a day (yes, four!), including a five-course gourmet dinner and moonlight buffet. When you're not eating, prepare to be occupied with showboat-style entertainment and calliope concerts. Each trip begins with a Captain's Champagne Welcome, and there's dancing nightly. If that's not enough, you can busy yourself with onboard lectures, planned activities, or craft lessons. And don't miss out on a chance to listen to the "Steamboatin' Riverlorian" as he shares tales of days gone by. Take in the beautiful sights as you drift along the Mississippi River, and when it's time to turn in, head to a Victorian-style cabin with all the modern amenities. Choose from the three-night to eleven-night cruises. Prices range from $600 to $7,000 depending on time of year and the destination. (800) 543-1949.

RiverBarge Excursion Lines. 201 Opelousas Avenue, New Orleans, LA 70114. What's the most scenic way to get to St. Louis? On a barge, of course. This six-day trip takes you on a tour of the upper and lower Mississippi River, highlighting its convergence with the Ohio River. Tour guides fill you in on the local history, including earthquakes and shipwrecks. Throughout the trip, you can relax while the ship banks for overnight stays in a variety of cities along the way, including Saint Genevieve and Cape Girardeau, Missouri, and Columbus, Kentucky. Call for schedules and prices, as well as a free brochure that outlines the itinerary. (888) GO-BARGE.

WEST MEMPHIS

From downtown Memphis, follow Front Street to the foot of the Hernando DeSoto Bridge. Once you cross the bridge, you've reached the home of Southland Greyhound Park—West Memphis's claim to fame. And when the hotels of downtown Memphis are filled because of conventions, many Memphians turn to the accommodations in West Memphis to house guests or to rest themselves. When you head home, be sure to fill your tank with gas: West Memphis boasts some of the lowest gas prices in the area. Perhaps that's why it's become the Trucker Capital of the United States.

WHERE TO GO

West Memphis Chamber of Commerce. 108 West Broadway Street, West Memphis, AR 72310. Before heading to the dog track or to one of West Memphis's fun outdoor events, stop by the chamber of commerce to gather information about the community. (870) 735-1134.

Southland Greyhound Park. 1550 North Ingram Boulevard, West Memphis, AR 72310. There's only one greyhound-racing facility in the Midsouth, and it's right across the bridge in West Memphis. This park boasts top purses and is the home of the leading racing greyhounds in the world. Southland Greyhound Park visitors won't miss out on any racing action because the park also has simulcast horse racing. Racing at Southland is year-round. Open from 11:00 A.M. to 1:00 A.M.; admission is free on the downstairs level. (870) 735-3670.

WHERE TO STAY

Comfort Inn. 1300 Ingram Boulevard Extension, West Memphis, AR 72310. The Comfort Inn offers fifty-two deluxe rooms, many of which come with microwaves and refrigerators. There's an outdoor pool and a complimentary continental breakfast available for all guests. (870) 732-0044.

Holiday Inn. I-55 and I-40 at Ingram Boulevard, West Memphis, AR 72310 This West Memphis Holiday Inn has more than 120 rooms and a full-service restaurant offering three meals daily. There's also an indoor pool and a video arcade to keep young travelers busy. (870) 735-1423; (800) HOLIDAY.

SPECIAL EVENTS

Main Street Fall Festival and Chili Cook-Off. October. Union Planters Plaza at the corner of Missouri and Broadway, West Memphis, AR. This fun family event features arts and crafts, live entertainment, and a special children's area. (870) 735-8814.

West Memphis Dickens of a Christmas. December. West Memphis Civic Complex, 200 West Polk Avenue, West Memphis, AR 72303. This month-long event features an array of holiday lights, the opening of the ice rink, a tour of the Dickens Village, as well as a number of holiday activities and Christmas performances. For more information, contact the West Memphis Convention and Visitor's Bureau. (870) 732-7598.

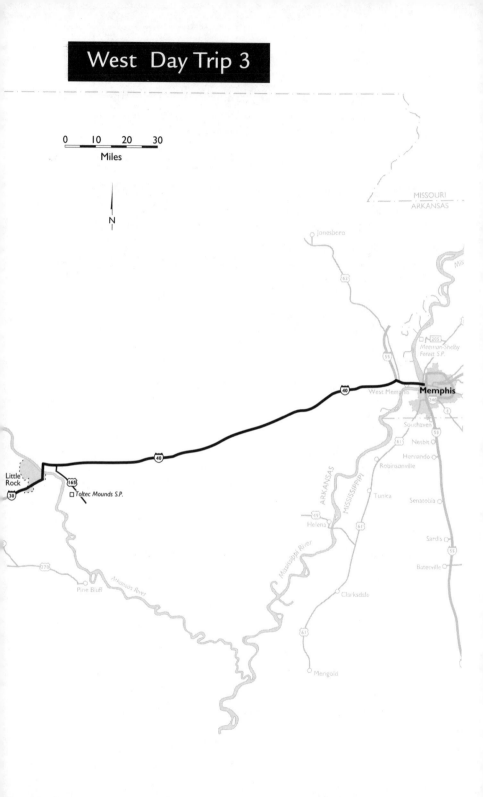

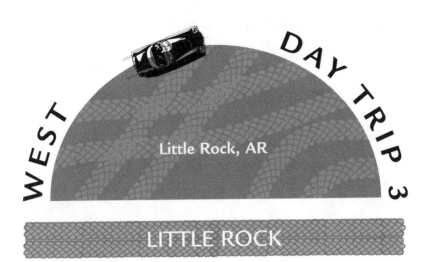

LITTLE ROCK

It's an easy drive from Memphis to Little Rock. Just take I-40 west (Poplar Avenue turns into I-40 downtown at the river). You'll cross the Mississippi and then head through West Memphis on your way to the Arkansas state capital. That's it. If you can think about all the fun you'll have once in Little Rock, it'll help you endure the bleak expanse of open, empty space you're driving through. Arkansas isn't very pretty from here to Little Rock, and there's not much to do on the way: just a few gas stations and fast-food joints. During the ride, though, you can begin to plan your day trip around the many attractions and restaurants that La Petite Roche has to offer. Incidentally, Little Rock gets its name from a mountainous rock that rests in the center of the city, making it both the literal and social focal point.

Because it's the state capital, there are plenty of touristy things to do, including several attractions for children like the Little Rock Zoo, the Children's Museum of Art, and the Museum of Discovery. Adults might find some of the shopping areas, especially the Heights and River Market, and art museums more interesting. Most midsoutherners know that Little Rock is also the former home and stomping ground of Bill and Hillary Clinton, and their names and reputations remain prominent fixtures in all parts of the city. You'll see Clinton Avenue stretching through the downtown area just a block from the Clinton-made-famous-by-way-of-Paula-Jones Excelsior Hotel. If you're lucky, you may even overhear some "established" Little Rock ladies whispering Clinton-era political secrets over tea in the lobby.

WHERE TO GO

Little Rock Convention and Visitors Bureau. Robinson Center at Markham and Broadway, Little Rock, AR 72201. At the visitors bureau, you can get information about every kind of tourist activity in Little Rock as well as lots of information about the surrounding area. (501) 376-4781; (800) 844-4781.

Little Rock Zoo. 1 Jonesboro Drive, Little Rock, AR 72205. The forty-acre Little Rock Zoo is easy to find, just off I-64 at exit 4. Once you're there, you'll find more than 600 animals from 170 species—both native and exotic, and some on the endangered list. There's a tropical rain forest for Amazon inhabitants as well as a big-cat habitat and a "Great Ape" exhibit, among other zoo attractions. Be sure to visit Anga, one of the only black rhinos in the world. There's a train station with miniature train for a quick ride and a Safari Trader Gift Shop for "zoo-venirs." If you arrive before 11:30 A.M. on the last Saturday of the month, entry is free. Open daily, except on major holidays. (501) 666-2406.

Children's Museum of Arkansas. 1400 West Markham #200, Little Rock, AR 72201. The Children's Museum is basically a huge interactive and educational playground for children of all ages. It's located in the former Union Station in the downtown area of the capital, within a few blocks of the River Market. In the interactive, hands-on part of the museum, kids build forts and mazes and other structures with interlocking bricks. But the highlight of the museum is its bubble center, where kids both young and old can blow nearly any kind of soap bubble imaginable: 5 feet high, square, one inside the other . . . the list goes on! Fee. Friday evening free. Closed Monday. (501) 374-6655.

Arkansas Arts Center. Ninth and Commerce Streets, MacArthur Park, Little Rock, AR 72203. The Arts Center is the largest cultural institution in the state of Arkansas and features many visual and performing arts exhibits and activities. The Arkansas Museum of Art is the most prominent of the MacArthur Park venues. Here you'll find a permanent world-class drawing collection dating back to the Renaissance. At the Decorative Arts Museum, located in the Pike-Fletcher-Terry House nearby, there's a fascinating collection of "heritage" artifacts, like quilts, silver, and jewelry. Particularly fun is the artistic toys exhibit. The children's theater has a fairly regular schedule of sophisticated but child-friendly plays, including *Little Women, Charlie and the Chocolate Factory, Beauty and the Beast,* and *The Mind of Leonardo da Vinci* for the older child. (501) 372-4000.

Aerospace Education Center. 3301 East Roosevelt Road, Little Rock, AR 72206. The Aerospace Center is appropriately located near the Little Rock National Airport. It's billed as the state's number one educational and entertainment attraction. There are several different venues here, including an IMAX theater, a library and memorabilia collection, and a permanent collection of aerospace artifacts—for example, an Apollo command and service module and an exact replica of the Wright Flyer. (501) 376-4232.

Toltec Mounds Archeological State Park. 490 Toltec Mounds Road, Scott, AR 72142. The Toltec Mounds are Arkansas's tallest Native American earthworks mounds, dating from A.D. 600 to A.D. 1050. They're located just fifteen minutes or so southeast of Little Rock: From I-440, the city's loop, exit onto I-165 and drive 9 miles to Toltec Road, then exit east to get to the park. In addition to the earthworks themselves—which you can tour on a 0.75-mile barrier-free trail—you'll find an interpretive center, including a visitor center, exhibits, a theater, and a research laboratory. Arkansas State Parks and the Archeological Survey manage the facilities. Nominal fee. (501) 961-9442.

Old State House Museum. 300 West Markham, Little Rock, AR 72201. Aptly named, the Old State House is a museum of Arkansas history from the time it became a state up through the present day, with special emphasis on the years between 1836 and 1911, when the building was the seat of the Arkansas government. The House considers itself a "multimedia museum of Arkansas history, people, and culture." Its interesting permanent exhibits include *"As Long as Life Shall Last": The Legacy of Arkansas Women; 1836 House of Representatives; The Clinton Exhibit: From the Old State House to the White House; First Families: The Mingling of Politics and Culture.* In addition to politics and history, changing exhibits often emphasize art. Free. Open daily except major holidays. www.oldstatehouse.org. (501) 324-9685 .

WHERE TO SHOP

The Heights. To get to the Heights, just head north on the main drag, Cantrell Road, and make a right onto Kavanaugh, which will wind around and plant you right in one of Little Rock's premier shopping neighborhoods. The Heights is bohemian in a sophisticated, trendy kind of way. You'll find art, gift, and jewelry galleries, like Chroma, Faux Pas, Dauphine, and Thomas; restaurants, such as Boulevard Bread Co., Browning's Mexican Restaurant, Café Prego (see below), and Spaulé; and even a spa, called Caracella's Hair and Body Salon. A particularly fun and eclectic boutique is Southern Image, where Little Rock "ladies" and college kids alike shop for everything from leopard-shaded lamps to faux fruit and children's accessories. The Heights represents Little Rock shopping at its mostest.

River Market. On a bluff over the Arkansas River in the downtown historic district is Little Rock's thriving new hub, River Market. It's a stone's throw from the Little Rock Peabody and runs along West Markham Street, which bustles with shopping and dining activity (see Where to Eat for restaurants on this strip). It's part of the district's renaissance, an effort to bring business and visitors to the downtown area, specifically Markham Street. It's definitely a marketplace: There are numerous restaurants, food stands, art galleries, clothing and gift boutiques, coffee shops, and pubs. Many come here just to window-shop, but most make the trek to River Market to pick and choose among the many avant-garde as well as traditional home accessories and chic, somewhat expensive clothing. The best part about shopping at River Market is the lunch break in the food emporium (or at any number of restaurants along Markham Street).

WHERE TO EAT

Cajun's Wharf. 2400 Cantrell Road, Little Rock, AR 72202. Located in the warehouse district not far from downtown is Cajun's Wharf restaurant and bar. Tell anyone in town you're going to Cajun's and they'll want to join you, especially if it's a Friday or Saturday night when the place is always hopping. In fact, it's often an hour wait just to get seated. But before settling in at a table for some gourmet seafood or surf and turf, you can meander into the restaurant's adjoining and always crowded bar. The restaurant portion of Cajun's is dimly lit, wooden-beamed, and warmed by the center fireplace. If you happen to get a table by the window, you'll be able to enjoy your meal as you watch the boats go by on the Arkansas River, which flows just a stone's throw away. The favorite dishes for regulars are the bacon-wrapped shrimp and the mixed seafood platter. The vegetables and rice with artichokes, served with most entrees, are superb. $$–$$$; ☐. (501) 375-5351.

Flying Saucer Draught Emporium. 323 East Markham Street, Little Rock, AR 72202. The Flying Saucer is primarily a "beer house," located right in the heart of the River Market area; this central locale makes it a frequent watering hole for both the postwork happy-hour crowd and visitors to the riverfront area. Inside you'll find a selection of literally hundreds of beers from all over the world—most on tap— and a ceiling covered with "saucers." Monday night is "pint night," when most beers are about half price; each day the featured beer ($2.50 per pint) changes. In addition to the hops, you get free popcorn and can order things like a sausage and cheese plate or bratwurst with sauerkraut from the German-inspired menu. It gets reasonably rowdy during happy hour and on weekend nights, when everyone stops in to play darts and checkers in the game area and listen to the live music while sipping their favorite brewski. $$; ☐. (501) 372-PINT.

Casa Manana Taquiera. 400 East Markham Street, Little Rock, AR 72201. Just across the street from the Flying Saucer, you'll find Casa Manana, a Tex-Mex restaurant. Margaritas are made in frozen drink machines and served in cactus-stemmed glasses. The menu has the standard choice of tacos, fajitas, salads, and burritos. One nice thing about Casa Manana is that if you've got a group, you can order a pound or more of fajitas, making your meal a real sharing experience. $$; ☐. (501) 372-6637.

Graffiti's. 7811 Cantrell Road, Little Rock, AR 72227. Graffiti's is a popular Little Rock hangout because of its laid-back atmosphere and can't-go-wrong variety of solid Italian cooking. Part of the reason it's so much fun is that the whole point of Graffiti's is graffiti: Patrons are invited to sign their tablecloth, to leave a message on the wall, and to doodle on the woodwork. Once you decide to order, you can choose from a list of nearly every conceivable Italian dish, including "lite" entrees, and a selection of Italian and California wines. Graffiti's offers its house wine by the half carafe (in addition to wine by the glass and bottle), making it easier to enjoy a white with your appetizer and a red with your main course. Menu items include Graffiti's Specialty (seafood fettuccine), veal osso buco or piccata, Latin chicken, and beef tenderloin. Locals dine here so often that there's even a section on the menu called "Your Favorites," which offers a variety of pastas both in half and full portions, including the extraordinary linguine with escargots. Complete your meal with the cappuccino frozen cream cheese torte with hot ambrosia chocolate sauce or a scoop of traditional Italian ice splashed with vodka. $$–$$$; ☐. (501) 224-9079.

Café Prego. 5510 Kavanaugh Boulevard, Little Rock, AR 72207. Little Rock natives have a special affection for Café Prego, and you will too after visiting this eclectic, cramped, but cozy dining spot up in the Heights. Part of the reason why diners love this place so much is because of Louis, the French owner who waits tables, cooks, and cleans up along with his wife. You'll even hear him giving orders in French to his sous-chef, but that's what makes Café Prego so inviting: It's a family affair. Of course, the food is good too. The menu is diverse and interesting, including a wide variety of Italian specialties, often given a French flair. $$; ☐. (501) 663-5355.

WHERE TO STAY

Little Rock Peabody Hotel. 3 Statehouse Plaza, Little Rock, AR 72201-1412. As this book goes to press, the Peabody Hotel is steeped in a total renovation, which will be finished in time for the new grand opening in December 2001. The hotel was recently purchased by Memphis-based Belz Enterprises (yes, the same Belz that own the Memphis Peabody). It's turning what was once the Excelsior Hotel into Little Rock's own version of the luxurious and duck-friendly resting spot. The lobby promises to have the same lush ambience—sweetly swimming ducks included—as its sister in Memphis, and the rooms are 100 percent new, including the beds and all the furnishings. As a guest, you'll bask in the glow of gold-leaf lighting fixtures and rest peacefully in the featherbedlike mattresses. And no matter which side of the hotel your room is on, you'll have a great view: either of the city itself or of the Arkansas River. Furthermore, at the Peabody, you'll also find all the amenities and services of a full-service hotel, including room service and an on-site restaurant and bar. The front desk can even arrange laundering, if you decide to hang out for longer than you'd planned. $$$; ☐. (501) 375-5005; (800) 527-1745.

The Rosemont Luxury Bed and Breakfast. 515 West 15th Street, Little Rock, AR 72202. If you want something more intimate than the grand, skyscraper Peabody, make your way to the city's downtown historic district, where the Governor's Mansion is, and you'll find the Rosemont. It's only five blocks from I-630, connecting with I-30 and I-40, so it's easy to get there. Once you arrive, the Italianate architecture, meandering wisteria, period furnishings, and elegantly simple decor will make you feel as though you've stepped back to the nineteenth century. Indeed, the inn was built in 1880 but completely renovated in 1999 before opening for business as the Rosemont in 2000. It's on the National Register of Historic Places.

The expressed first priority of Susan Payne Maddox, the innkeeper, is to "indulge" you with "outrageous luxury." She wants you to profoundly enjoy your escape from the hectic pace of everyday life. At the Rosemont, there are five guest rooms, all with private bath, as well as a suite that accommodates a third person in the adjoining sleeping porch. Some rooms even have a fireplace and/or Jacuzzi for ultimate relaxing. Begin your day with a full breakfast served in the dining room or in the privacy of your own room (on request), take a midday break swinging or rocking on the front porch with a lemonade, and end it with an on-the-house glass of wine or beer and snack. Call for information on the Rosemont Romance package. $$; ☐. (501) 374-7456.

The Empress of Little Rock. 2120 Louisiana, Little Rock, AR 72206. It's double the price, but it's double the experience. The Empress of Little Rock is fit for a queen—or an empress, as the case may be. You'll catch your breath as you approach this enchanting Victorian mansion, which was originally built as a saloon in 1888 by James Hornibrook. In 1897 it became the home of the state's first Arkansas Women's College; after the depression the Hornibrook served as a private residence and apartments. But in 1995 it was completely restored and turned into the Empress inn. It's listed on the National Register of Historic Places and located in the Quapaw Quarter historic district.

The Empress is the kind of place you dream about: The 64-foot stained-glass window, sweeping double staircase, turreted watch tower, traditional nineteenth-century drawing room, claw-footed tubs, and luxurious antiques all beckon you to imagine the slow elegance of days gone by. When you arrive, hosts Robert Blair and Sharon Welch-Blair invite you to "cross the threshold to 1888" as they take you on a tour of the mansion and show you to your room with private parlor and bath. In the morning they'll treat you to a candelit gourmet breakfast. Visit the Web site to find out about special packages. The Empress is also the only inn in Arkansas to receive AAA's Four-Diamond award. $$$; ☐. www.theempress.com/. (501) 374-7966; (877) 374-7966.

Baker House. 109 West Fifth Street, Little Rock, AR 72114. Because of its location at Fifth and Main Streets in Little Rock's downtown historic district, the Baker House has been an integral part of this area's renaissance. The inn itself was built in 1899 as a boardinghouse for travelers and railroad workers alike. The architecture, decor, and furnishings are Victorian in style and explain why the house is listed on the National Register of Historic Places. As you enter, you'll see a beautifully appointed parlor, enlivened with bounteous floral displays. If you listen carefully, you'll hear the sounds of a Porter music box floating from the second parlor. The innkeeper, Justin Albright, will take you up the circular staircase and show you to your room.

Here's what's in store for you: the Tucker Suite—described by the inn as "regal"—offers you the luxury of sleeping on the king-sized tobacco leaf bed; the Decantillion Suite holds only a double bed, but guests can enjoy the suite's private Jacuzzi; and upstairs, the spacious Argenta Suite gives guests ultimate privacy with its own sitting area, adorned with carved antique mantels. There are a couple of other rooms, including one with two twin beds. If you're interested in venturing out of your room, visit the inn's library, located in the top-floor widow's walk, where the home's mistress once watched the Arkansas River for her husband to arrive. $$-$$$; ☐. (501) 372-1268; (888) 298-0255

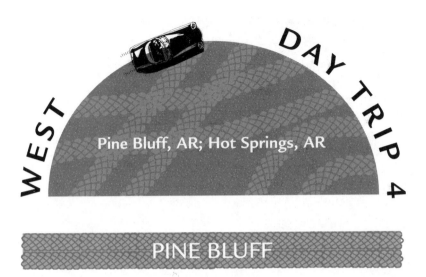

PINE BLUFF

Although it's a bit farther from Memphis than other destinations in this book, Pine Bluff is a town you won't want to overlook. Viewed as one of the premier art districts in Arkansas, Pine Bluff offers a multicultural experience for tourists of all ages. From downtown Memphis, merge onto I-40 west. At West Memphis I-40 turns southwest toward Little Rock. Merge onto I-30 west. Take exit 138B, then merge onto US 65/167 south. Take exit 35, toward Pine Bluff, continuing on US 65.

The history of the Pine Bluff area is as colorful as the artwork found in this town. The first settler was Joseph Bonne, a man who was half French and half Quapaw Indian. He built his log-cabin home on the high bluff around the early 1800s, and it quickly became known as the Pine Bluff, due to the fact that it was the first bluff supporting pine trees upstream from the mouth of the Arkansas River. The settlement grew and became incorporated as "The Town of Pine Bluff" on January 8, 1839. Since its inception, Pine Bluff endured the battle of Pine Bluff during the Civil War. On October 25, 1863, Confederate troops invaded the area, but Lieutenant M.F. Clark announced there would be no surrender and slowly forced the Confederates into Pine Bluff. Meanwhile, in town, about 300 African American soldiers barricaded the town square with cotton bales and protected the town's prized square. The Confederates were forced to retreat. Today, Pine Bluff draws visitors from all around.

155

West Day Trip 4

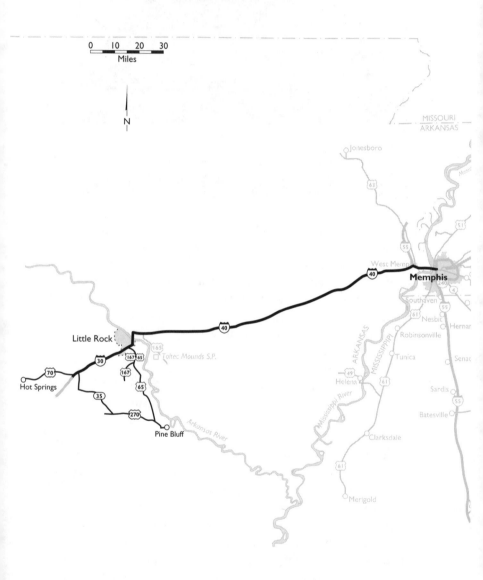

WHERE TO GO

Pine Bluff Convention & Visitors Bureau. 1 Convention Center Plaza, Pine Bluff, AR 71601. The Pine Bluff Convention & Visitors Bureau boasts more than 90,000 square feet of meeting and exhibit space, making it one of the largest meeting facilities in Arkansas. This immense center features an arena, auditorium/theater, a number of meeting rooms, plenty of parking, full camper hook-ups, and a beautiful park that's perfect for outdoor activities. (870) 536-7600.

The Arkansas Entertainers Hall of Fame. 1 Convention Center Plaza, Pine Bluff, AR 71601. Located inside the Pine Bluff Convention Center, the Arkansas Entertainers Hall of Fame opened in 1998 and pays tribute to famous Arkansas entertainers. When visitors stop by, they're greeted by a life-sized talking animatronic statue of Johnny Cash. The museum currently features twenty-seven inductees, including Art Porter Sr., Lum & Abner, Mary Steenburgen, Al Green, the Browns, Randy Goodrum, Tracy Lawrence, Wayland Holyfield, Levon Helm, Charlie Rich, and Conway Twitty—and there's still room to grow. Many well-known Arkansas entertainers, performing and nonperforming, who have been inducted into the Hall of Fame have contributed personal and professional artifacts from their careers in the limelight. Admission is free. (870) 536-7600.

Jefferson County Historical Museum. 201 East Fourth Street, Pine Bluff, AR 71601. The Jefferson County Historical Museum displays memorabilia collected over the centuries from famous events in the Pine Bluff area. Visitors can view a wide array of tools, relics, and cotton-farming implements from before the turn of the twentieth century. There's also a collection of Victorian furniture, antique dolls, and an exposition of period clothing that gives visitors insight into the lives of Jefferson County residents in times gone by. The museum features a wide collection of Civil War artifacts as well. It's located at the Union Station train depot, which has been restored and is listed on the National Register of Historic Places. Open daily, and admission is free. (870) 541-5402.

Old District of Pine Bluff Historic Home Tours. 1 Convention Center Plaza, Pine Bluff, AR 71601. Pine Bluff offers a number of historic homes, each flawlessly restored to near-original condition.

The tour departs from the Convention and Visitors Bureau (870-536-7600). Stops along the way include:

Dexter Harding House. 110 Pine Street, Pine Bluff, AR 71601. Begin your tour at this fascinating home that was built around 1850. It also serves as a visitor information center for the Old District of Pine Bluff. Open Tuesday through Saturday, from 10:00 A.M. to 4:00 P.M.

Ben Pearson Home. 716 West Barraque Street, Pine Bluff, AR 71601. This Victorian-style home was once the dwelling place of the famous archer, bowhunter, and manufacturer Ben Pearson. It features an interesting display of memorabilia reflecting the sportsmanship of its previous owner.

DuBocage Home. 1115 West Fourth Avenue, Pine Bluff, AR 71601. This residence is the former home of Judge Joseph W. and Frances Lindsay Bocage and is listed on the National Register of Historic Places. Built around 1860, the house was restored in 1970.

Martha Mitchell Home. West Fourth and Elm, Pine Bluff, AR 71601. Built circa 1887, this house was the birthplace (and later residence) of the outspoken wife of former U.S. Attorney General John Mitchell in the Nixon administration.

Trinity Episcopal Church. 703 West Third Street, Pine Bluff, AR 71601. Built in the mid-1800s, this is Arkansas's oldest Episcopal church. Some of the most prominent features include the Gothic architecture and the stained-glass windows, with reflections of its nineteenth-century construction found throughout the structure.

Japanese Gardens. 500 Eighth Street, Pine Bluff, AR 71601. Donated to the town of Pine Bluff by its sister city—Iwai, Japan—the Japanese Gardens are quite a unique attraction for the area. Pine Bluff is the only city in Arkansas to have such a garden, which features a walking tour and description of the unique foliage and rock gardens. (870) 536-7600.

Arkansas Railroad Museum. US 65, Pine Bluff, AR 71601. Weighing in at 368 tons and measuring 100 feet from front to back, engine 819 has earned quite a spot in Arkansas history. This "legendary queen of steam" requires 150 gallons of water and 15 gallons of oil just to get started down the tracks. But today she rests at the Arkansas Railroad Museum in Pine Bluff. She sits along side a host of other railway memorabilia, all housed in the vintage store-fronts of the Cotton Belt Railway. This immense collection of shops once kept engines and rail cars moving along an enormous rail system that ran throughout the South. The Arkansas Railroad Museum is open Monday through Saturday from 8:30 A.M. to 2:30 P.M. Special tours can be arranged by contacting the visitor bureau. (870) 536–8819.

The Band Museum. 423–425 Main Street, Pine Bluff, AR 71601. For those who've experienced the joy of playing with the band (or for those who've always wanted to), this museum is a must-see. It's the only museum in the United States devoted to band instruments and the history of the band movement in America. The museum boasts a collection of hundreds of vintage and antique band instruments dating back as far as the early 1700s. There's a collection of instruments owned by famous band musicians, as well as rare photos. Additionally, the museum features an astonishing variety of brass, percussion, and woodwind instruments. The museum itself is located within a historic down-town building erected in 1890. It's open daily, and admission is free. (870) 534–HORN (4676).

The Arts and Science Center for Southeast Arkansas. 701 Main Street, Pine Bluff, AR 71601. The center features more than 20,000 square feet of fun and learning with a focus on visual and performing arts as well as the sciences. The Arts and Science Center features three art galleries, a science gallery, a theater, and a studio classroom. In addition, there are four areas where exhibits on art and science rotate throughout the year. And don't miss the Catherine M. Bellany Theatre, a 232-seat structure that promises to entertain you with both dramatic and musical productions year-round. The galleries can be visited at no charge; guided tours led by docents are available by reservation. If your group has more than fifteen people, please call to ensure that space is available in the galleries at the time you plan to visit. (870) 536–3375.

Leedell Moorehead–Graham Fine Arts Gallery. 1200 North University Drive, Pine Bluff, AR 71601. Sustained by the art depart-ment at the University of Arkansas at Pine Bluff, this gallery features *Keepers of the Spirit,* a series of twenty-five panels on continuous display. These panels walk visitors through the university's 120-year history through a variety of art forms and takes a look at the black experience within the university as well. A monthly rotation of exhibits by regional and national artists is also on display in the east wing of the gallery. The gallery is open 8:30 A.M. to 4:30 P.M., Monday through Friday, and on weekends and evenings for groups by appointment. (870) 543–8236.

Murals of Pine Bluff. Downtown Pine Bluff, AR. Throughout downtown you'll find quite a display of artwork paying tribute to this bustling community. To date twelve murals have been painted in the area, offering visitors a chance to see the history of the town over the past 200 years. Because of this prominent display of artwork, Pine Bluff has earned itself the title of City of Murals.

Old Town Theatre Centre. 207 West Second Street, Pine Bluff, AR 71601. The Old Town Theatre Centre project focuses on the restoration and preservation of the Saenger Theatre, as well as the sustenance of the Community Theatre Museum in downtown Pine Bluff. The Saenger Theatre is home to the annual Pine Bluff Film Festival, held the first weekend of October. This festival pays tribute to silent films, while the Pine Bluff Symphony plays each film's original musical score. The Community Theatre Museum is the oldest one-screen theater still operating in Arkansas. It shows vintage films, hosts a lecture series, and offers "Wednesday Off Main," a variety of discounted performances, each week. (870) 434–8880

WHERE TO STAY

Margland Bed and Breakfast. 703 West Third Street, Pine Bluff, AR 71601. Built in the early 1900s, Margland raises the bar when it comes to bed-and-breakfasts. Each room is filled with warm, personal touches and exquisite antiques. Many bedrooms are loft-style, and an exercise room is available for guests. Private baths and Jacuzzis are available; each room comes with cable TV. Many guests linger in the shaded courtyard and walk through the garden. In spring and summer patrons can take a dip in the outdoor pool. (800) 545–5383.

Best Western Pines. 2700 East Harding, Pine Bluff, AR 71601. In addition to more than a hundred spacious standard rooms with cable television and air-conditioning, the Best Western Pine has a sauna and outdoor pool. A meeting and banquet room is also available; with advance notice, a courtesy car service is available for your trip to or from the airport. $$-$$$; ☐. (870) 535-8640.

Hampton Inn. 3103 East Market Street, Pine Bluff, AR 71601. Conveniently located across the street from the Pines Mall, this Hampton Inn is an easy and accessible place to rest. Connecting rooms and cribs are available for those traveling in a group or with children. Each room comes with a coffeepot and hair dryer. There's a pool on the premises. And keep in mind that pets aren't allowed. $$-$$$; ☐. (870) 850-0444; (800) HAMPTON.

HOT SPRINGS

If you're stressed from work or just looking for a beautiful vacation spot, Hot Springs—known for its natural hot-water geysers and incredible parks—is the place for you. To get there, follow I-40 west toward Little Rock. Merge onto I-30 west. Take exit 111 to Hot Springs.

The thermal waters that gave Hot Springs its name are some of nature's most incredible works. There are more than forty-seven springs along the forested southwestern slope of Hot Springs Mountain. Every day, these springs emit almost one million gallons of water that reaches 143 degrees. The water has been carbon-dated by scientists who believe it to be the result of major rains in the central Arkansas forests over 4,000 years ago. All that water slowly penetrated the earth's crust and seeped into the earth's core, which forced it to surge to the surface through these hot springs. At one time these springs were used as a source of medicines treating arthritis and a number of other ailments and diseases. Today they make for one of the most relaxing destinations in the world.

WHERE TO GO

Hot Springs National Park. 369 Central Avenue, Hot Springs, AR 71901. This is one of the most fascinating parks anywhere. The smallest and oldest park in the National Park System, it dates back to 1832. Originally called Hot Springs Reservation, it was renamed in 1921. Don't be misled by its size; there's plenty to discover in this national park.

A winding drive up Hot Springs Mountain behind the bathhouses takes you to scenic Hot Springs Mountain Tower, where you can take elevators to the top of the mountain and enjoy a dramatic view of the city, mountains, forests, and lakes that surround Hot Springs for 40 miles in each direction. On the northern side of the mountain is lovely Gulpha Gorge Campground, which offers camping amenities in a shaded and serene natural setting on the banks of Gulpha Creek. There's also a 26-mile network of hiking trails that range from the easily maneuvered Grand Promenade to some difficult rugged mountain treks across the park.

Continue your visit with a stop at the luxuriously restored Fordyce Bathhouse, positioned in the center of world-famous Bathhouse Row. You will be transported back to a different time when Hot Springs "Bathed the World." Guided and self-guided tours through this marvelous structure will give you a rapid understanding of where the thermal waters come from, how they're used, and how the federal government supervises the use of the 800,000 gallons of hot water that gush uninterrupted from the earth each day. Along the way, there are display springs that let you feel just how hot the water really is, and you can rest your feet in the beautiful cascade of thermal water at the northern end of Bathhouse Row while you enjoy the scenery of Arlington Lawn Park. At the southern end of Bathhouse Row is Buckstaff Bathhouse, which is operated under the supervision of the park service in the same way many of the other bathhouses were in their prime. (501) 624-3383.

Hot Springs bathhouses. The bathhouses of Hot Springs are probably the most popular tourist attraction in town. What better way to spend an afternoon than by unwinding with an invigorating and rejuvenating thermal bath? Try any of these locations for a hot mineral-water bath and massage:

> **The Arlington.** 239 Central Avenue, Hot Springs, AR 71901. The Arlington Bath House boasts a skilled staff of attendants and massage therapists who aim to please as they pamper guests with thermal whirlpool baths, hot packs, and massages. These treatments are sure to relax body and mind while they soothe arthritis, neuritis, circulatory problems, and just plain aching muscles. Hours of operation are as follows: Monday through Wednesday from 7:00 to 11:30 A.M. and 1:30 to 5:00 P.M.; Thursday through

Saturday from 7:00 to 11:30 A.M. and 1:30 to 9:00 P.M.; Sunday from 7:00 A.M. to noon. www.arlingtonhotel.com. (501) 623-7771; (800) 643-1502.

Austin Hotel and Convention Center. 305 Malvern Avenue, Hot Springs, AR 71901. The Austin is located in historic downtown Hot Springs right beside the Hot Springs Civic and Convention Center. You don't have to be a guest to take part in the pleasure of a relaxing mineral soak—reservations are accepted. Hours of operation are Monday through Friday from 8:00 A.M. to 1:00 P.M. and 3:00 P.M. to 8:00 P.M. www.theaustinhotel.com. (501) 623-6600; (800) 844-7275.

Buckstaff Bathhouse Company. 509 Central Avenue, Hot Springs, AR 71901. Dating to 1912, the Buckstaff Bathhouse is the only remaining continuously run traditional thermal bathing facility on Bathhouse Row. Visitors can indulge in mineral baths, hot packs, sitz baths, steam cabinets, and Swedish massages. And best of all, no reservations are needed. The Buckstaff is open Monday through Saturday. (501) 623-2308.

The Majestic Resort and Spa. 101 Park Avenue, Hot Springs, AR 71902. The Majestic Spa features Hot Springs' world-famous thermal mineral baths, as well as whirlpools, heat packs, and massages. Hours of operation are as follows: Monday through Friday, 7:00 to 11:30 A.M. and 4:30 to 9:00 P.M.; Saturday 7:00 to 11:30 A.M. and 1:30 to 9:00 P.M.; Sunday 7:00 to 11:30 A.M. www.themajestichotel.com. (501) 623-5511; (800) 643-1504.

Swan Song Spa. 504 Park Avenue, Hot Springs, AR 71901. In addition to traditional services, the Swan Song Spa also features private and co-ed water spa and Jacuzzi baths. It's open Thursday through Monday. www.swansongspa.com. (501) 623-5597; (888) 588-6663.

Clowers' World Famous Zoo with I.Q. 380 Whittington Avenue, Hot Springs, AR 71901. The I.Q. Zoo was started in 1955 by Dr. Keller Breland and has featured continuous animal shows since its inception. Today it's owned by Jim Clowers, one of the few remaining trainers taught by Breland. The zoo is filled with trained animals who entertain based on popular movie themes. For example, Luke Sky Hopper the space rabbit, Greaser chicken from Rydell High, and Bat Pig are all on hand to show off for audiences. In 1999 Roadside America ranked the Zoo with I.Q. the number one roadside attraction in the nation. It's open daily from 10:00 A.M. to 3:00 P.M., and there is an admission charge. (501) 623-9695.

Maxwell Blade's Theatre of Magic. 817 Central Avenue, Hot Springs, AR 71901. The thrill of a Las Vegas show comes to downtown Hot Springs when Maxwell Blade performs his magic and illusions. This "master of illusion" has performed for audiences throughout the world and his ninety-minute performance includes a mysterious choreographed plot. The show is complete with lighting, sound, and incredible costumes. Guests of all ages can enjoy performances four nights a week at the historic Malco Theatre. The show begins at 8:00 P.M.; group rates are available. www.hotspringsar.com/blade. (501) 623-6200.

Music Mountain Jamboree. 1555 East Grand Avenue, Hot Springs, AR 71901. The Music Mountain Jamboree has been rated Hot Springs' number one musical comedy stage show for the past nineteen seasons. This performance is housed in a 650-seat theater, so bring the family and enjoy some knee-slapping, foot-stomping good music along with good, clean comedy. Performances vary throughout the year. (501) 609-9700.

The Bath House Show. 701 Central Avenue, Hot Springs, AR 71901. The Bath House Show mixes great music from the past six decades with a hearty dose of humor. This two-hour production includes a performance from the internationally acclaimed "Buford Presley." Make reservations for this comical treat in downtown Hot Springs. (501) 623-1415.

The Pocket Theatre. 2138 Higdon Ferry Road, Hot Springs, AR 71901. This is the only area theater that boasts live, year-round performances. Shows and times change regularly, so call before coming, or visit the Web site: www.pockettheatre.com. (501) 525-PLAY (7529).

The Witness. 1960 Millcreek Road, Hot Springs, AR 71902. The Witness Amphitheater, located on the beautiful Panther Valley Ranch, reenacts "the Greatest Story Ever Told"—the birth, life, death, and resurrection of Jesus Christ as seen through the eyes of the disciple Peter. This Hot Springs musical passion play takes place

June through October every Friday and Saturday night at dusk, plus a special performance on Sunday night of the Labor Day weekend. Call for reservations. (501) 623-9781.

Magic Springs & Crystal Falls. 1701 Highway 70 East, Hot Springs, AR 71901. Magic Springs claims that you'll find a ride for you here "whether you like your thrills mild or intense." And with more than seventy-five to chose from, they can't be wrong. Once you've ridden all you can, relax at Crystal Falls Water Park. Magic Springs & Crystals Falls is open rain or shine, but call in advance for hours and prices. (501) 624-0100.

Castleberry Riding Stables. 537 Walnut Valley Road, Hot Springs, AR 71901. Castleberry is a family-owned and -operated stable that has been around for more than thirty-five years. It offers guided mountain trail horseback riding for guests of all ages. The tour takes you through the tree-shaded woods located on the north side of Blow Out Mountain. You'll also get to feel like you're in the Old West as you cross two streams and a large spring-fed pond stocked with large catfish. And to complete the western experience, Castleberry Riding Stables offers a breakfast ride, where you can enjoy a meal prepared over an open hickory fire and served on the banks of the pond. If you bring a large group, you can take part in a hayride, cookout, or retreat. The stable is open year-round, weather permitting. (501) 623-6609.

Arkansas Alligator Farm & Petting Zoo. 847 Whittington Avenue, Hot Springs, AR 71901. The Arkansas Alligator Farm & Petting Zoo has been ranked one of the best wildlife sanctuaries in the United States by *Good Housekeeping* magazine, and it's no wonder. You'll find more than 300 alligators ranging from 6 inches to 10 feet long, along with a petting zoo that houses deer, pygmy goats, llamas, lambs, and ostriches. In the museum part of the zoo, tourists can see a wide variety of monkeys, mountain lions, and giant turtles, as well as the "Mer-Man" creature, which has been featured on the television show *That's Incredible* and in Ripley's Believe It or Not. The Arkansas Alligator Farm & Petting Zoo is open year-round. (501) 623-6172; (800) 750-7891.

Josephine Tussaud Wax Museum. 250 Central Avenue, Hot Springs, AR 71901. Experience an unending sense of intrigue when you walk through the doors of the Tussaud Wax Museum. Take your time and wander through the Seven Magic Worlds as you journey back in time. The latest additions to the museum are life-sized replicas of the Clintons. Don't forget to bring your camera. The museum is open seven days a week, and there's a fee. (501) 623-5836.

Mid-America Science Museum. 500 Mid-America Boulevard, Hot Springs, AR 71913. This museum offers a hands-on approach to the world of energy, life, matter, and perception. As the museum boasts, you can spend the day learning while you "pull, tug, push, spin, pump, and twist your way through the vast array of mind-boggling displays!" The museum is open from Memorial Day to Labor Day, from 9:30 A.M. to 6:00 P.M. seven days a week. During the rest of the year, it is open from 10:00 A.M. to 5:00 P.M. Tuesday through Sunday. Admission for children ages four through twelve is $5.00; for adults, it's $6.00. (501) 767-3461; (800) 632-0583.

National Park Aquarium. 209 Central Avenue, Hot Springs, AR 71901. The National Park Aquarium houses Arkansas's largest fish and reptile exhibit. On display are all kinds of native Arkansas fish, as well as many saltwater species, all in their natural habitats. In addition, you'll find an assortment of reptiles and a ninety-pound snapping turtle. The aquarium is open year-round, and there's an admission fee. www.hotspringsusa.com/aquarium. (501) 624-3474

WHERE TO SHOP

Artists' Galleria. 323 East Grand Avenue, Hot Springs, AR 71901. This hot spot for art offers a wide selection of works by Thomas H. Payne, as well as more traditional paintings from a variety of artists. (501) 624-7366.

Blue Moon Gallery. 718 Central Avenue, Hot Springs, AR 71901. This magical studio features a wide array of decorative pieces and sculptures. Open Monday through Saturday and by appointment. (501) 318-2787.

Golden Leaves Art Gallery and Book Store. 201 Malvern, Hot Springs, AR 71910. Golden Leaves is a must on your shopping excursion in Hot Springs. The gallery features art with Indian, Celtic, and European influences; the bookstore offers not just reading material, but also a large selection of incense. This is the perfect spot to select a gift by which to remember your trip to Hot Springs. (501) 623-7007.

WHERE TO EAT

Kozy Sports Bar & Grill. 1218 Airport Road, Hot Springs, AR 71901. Before you spend a quiet day at the baths, you might want to swing by Kozy Sports Bar & Grill to get the mischief out of your system. The spot offers typical bar fare, and tempts visitors to test their competitive side with pool tables, darts, and shuffleboard. $$; ☐. (501) 767–1488.

The French Market Café. 1538 Malvern Avenue, Hot Springs, AR 71901. This cafe is located inside the Indiandale Shopping Center and features a tempting menu of New Orleans–style cuisine. The French Market Café is open for lunch every day except Saturday and Monday. $$; ☐. (501) 623–2222.

Belle Arti Ristorante. 719 Central Avenue, Hot Springs, AR 71901. The Belle Arti is just about five blocks and a leisurely evening stroll from the Arlington Hotel—and you get to enjoy the view of Bathhouse Row as you go. Sit in the lower dining room, which is quite elegant with white tablecloths, flowers, and live piano music. If all the seats are taken, the hostess will take you upstairs, where you'll enjoy a less formal but more intimate setting. Although the menu boasts a wide range of Italian dishes, including veal, chicken, and seafood, the real draw is the pasta. Your waiter will also surely inform you that they have the best wine list in all of Hot Springs. $$–$$$; ☐. (501) 624–7474.

The Pancake House. 719 Central Avenue, Hot Springs, AR 71901. Everyone who's been to the Pancake House raves about this little breakfast diner, tucked into the row of shops just across from the Arlington Hotel. The menu favorites are whole-grain buckwheat pancakes, with or without blueberries, and the sausage, which is homemade from Arkansas pigs (a fact your waitress won't hesitate to mention). The rest of the menu is standard breakfast food: eggs, bacon, buttermilk pancakes. Be sure to order the freshly squeezed orange juice. Either while you're waiting for a table or after you've eaten, wander through the diner's adjoining gourmet food shop, with specialty marmalades, mustards, and salad dressings available for purchase. $. (501) 624–7474.

Back Porch Grill. 4801 Central Avenue, Hot Springs, AR 71901. Don't miss out on the beautiful view and live entertainment available at the Back Porch Grill. Positioned with a deck by the lake, the Back Porch is a great spot to hang out and listen to music. The menu features a number of incredible steak dinners, including a fabulous beef Wellington. The Back Porch also offers fresh seafood specials and vegetarian dishes. $$–$$$; ☐. (501) 525-0885.

WHERE TO STAY

The Arlington Resort Hotel & Spa. 239 Central Avenue, Hot Springs, AR 71901. This award-winning resort in the scenic Ouachita Mountains offers 481 rooms and suites, each professionally decorated. Many of the rooms have the mineral water that has made Hot Springs famous piped in directly. The Arlington also has its own bathhouse, where guests can be transported in a private elevator to the facilities for a relaxing mineral-water whirlpool bath and massage. In the Beauty and Facial Salon, guests can treat themselves to a number of services, including half or full days of treatment, Remy Laure facials, body masques, and mudpacks. And the Arlington doesn't overlook fine dining, with a variety of restaurants to choose from. You might select the continental menu and romantic setting of the Fountain Room Grill, or enjoy breakfast, brunch, and buffets in the Venetian Dining Room (complete with Old World charm). For tasty, light lunches, patrons often stop in the Lobby Café, and for dancing and entertainment, they turn to the Lobby Bar. If you stay at the Arlington, don't miss out on the great spa packages. $$–$$$; ☐. www.thearlingtonresort.com. (800) 643-1502.

The Majestic. 101 Park Avenue, Hot Springs, AR 71601. Since 1882 the Majestic has offered travelers the best in accommodations. Located in the heart of Hot Springs, this newly restored facility has not only 250 incredible rooms and suites to choose from but also a resort and spa complex, restaurants, on-premises thermal baths, a heated pool, and full golf and tennis privileges at Hot Springs Country Club. You'll find a stately fare at the daily breakfast buffet, or enjoy a memorable dinner in the Grady Manning Dining Room. For a bistro experience and full bar service, check out Grady's Grill Steak House and Wine Bar, which offers Black Angus steaks, seafood, and delicious desserts. Slip into days gone by as you enter the Ole' Fashion Soda Fountain, where fountain creations and refreshments are served. $$–$$$; ☐. (800) 643-1504.

The Gables Inn. 318 Quapaw Avenue, Hot Springs, AR 71901. The Gables Inn offers not only numerous gables but also a wraparound front porch and a number of stained-glass windows—it's a most romantic getaway. This immaculately restored 1905 Victorian home is filled with family treasures and offers four luxurious rooms, one which features a heart-shaped whirlpool tub for two. The innkeepers have thought of everything, including an emergency contact page you can print off their Web site and leave with friends and family. So leave your worries behind and sit a spell on the porch of this charming bed-and-breakfast. In the evening snack on the daily dessert selection. And when you're ready to leave, don't forget to stop by the gift shop and pick up an item by which to remember your trip. $$; ☐. (501) 623-7576; (800) 625-7576.

1890 Williams House. 420 Quapaw Avenue, Hot Springs, AR 71901. This unique bed-and-breakfast is a peaceful escape from the excitement of Hot Springs. All five of the rooms in the main house have 12-foot ceilings, beautiful woodwork, gorgeous antique decor, a sitting area, and a private bath; three of them offer whirlpool tubs for two. Every room also comes with a queen-sized bed, cable TV, VCR, air-conditioning, and a ceiling fan for those cool nightly breezes. For convenience you'll find an iron and ironing board, clock, hair dryer, soap, and shampoo in your room as well. The 1890 Williams House features two two-bedroom suites if you're traveling with a group. And a full-scale breakfast is served each morning. $$$; ☐. (501) 624-4275; (800) 756-4635.

SPECIAL EVENTS

Wine, Food, and Art Extravaganza. May. The annual Wine, Food, and Art Extravaganza is held on historic Bathhouse Row in downtown Hot Springs. Eight bathhouses, thirty-three wineries, nine chefs, and six art galleries combine their talents to benefit the Friends of the Fordyce and Hot Springs National Park. This is the only time of the year the bathhouses are open to the public.

Taste of Downtown Festival. May. This annual festival in downtown Hot Springs offers visitors musical entertainment, concessions, displays of goods by local merchants, exhibits, children's games, Hoopfest preliminaries, magic shows, a pie-eating contest, and more. (501) 321-2113.

Hot Springs Music Festival. June. A unique format unites promising young musicians from across the United States with accomplished mentors who work with them on classical music that spans the spectrum. Free performances and other performances that charge only a modest fee are sprinkled at locations all around Hot Springs throughout the festival. (501) 623-4763.

Hot Springs Street Art Festival. September. This incredible display of local crafstmanship is held each year at Hill Wheatly Plaza. (501) 624-6591.

Hot Springs Jazz Festival. September. This two-day jazz festival allows up-and-coming musicians to join the ranks of a number of veterans from the South like Herb Ellis and Mose Allison for a free jam. (501) 525-0228; (501) 922-4570.

Arkansas Senior Olympic Games. September. Athletes ages fifty and over from all over the United States gather in the Valley of the Vapors for competition in a number of events. The Arkansas competition is a qualifying site for the National Senior Olympics and sponsored by Senior Arkansas Sports.

Spa City Blues Festival. October. The Spa City Blues Society's Blues Festival always includes a full lineup of local, regional, and national musicians. In previous years bands such as Mike Morgan & the Crawl, the Blue Boogie Band, the Spa City Jammers, and others have hit the stage.

Hot Springs Documentary Film Festival. October. It's the Sundance of the South—Academy Award-winning documentarians from all over the globe head to Hot Springs to show their films, conduct classes and lectures, and visit with those in attendance. (501) 321-4747.

Arkansas Oktoberfest. October. Year after year, the Arkansas Oktoberfest at the Hot Springs Civic & Convention Center is ranked as one of the best such celebrations in the country. Come see why as Arkansans pay tribute to all things German, from an alpenhorn concert to knackwurst and a traditional beer garden. Eating and drinking aside, there's also a race, parade, dog show, crafts show, and horseshoe tournament. (501) 321-1700.

Sportsfest. November. Join in with hundreds of others taking part in an array of healthy activities, including a 5K or 10K run, a mountain bike challenge, and seminars from fitness authorities discussing the latest trends in the fields of health. For information on the running events, call (800) 713-7837. For the biking events, call (501) 623-6188.

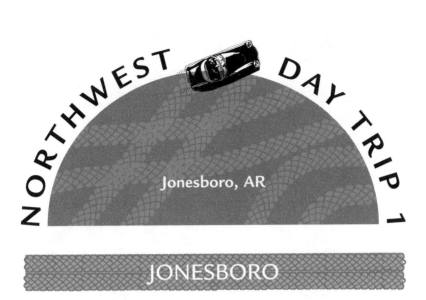

Jonesboro, AR

JONESBORO

From downtown Memphis, jump onto I–55 north (you can also get to I–55 by circling the city on I–240). The interstate will take you over the Mississippi River and into West Memphis; keep driving northwest about forty-five minutes until you hit US 63, exit 23B. Head in the direction of Jonesboro. US 63 changes names a few times, but if you keep your eye on the signs, you'll be fine. All in all, it'll take you about an hour and a half. Nearby is Lake Frierson State Park, offering visitors a breathtaking view of blooming dogwoods in spring and great fishing the rest of the year. Just northeast of Jonesboro proper is Arkansas State University. Because ASU is so close, much of the otherwise fairly sleepy town of Jonesboro relies on the college's cultural and social activities. To get to the university, simply take US 49 north, go right onto AR 230, and right again onto AR 135.

WHERE TO GO

Greater Jonesboro Chamber of Commerce. 1709 East Nettleton, Jonesboro, AR 72403. The chamber in Jonesboro can provide you with maps and information about the area. (870) 932–6691.

   Lake Frierson State Park. 7904 Highway 141, Jonesboro, AR 72401. This 135-acre park is located just 10 miles north of Jonesboro on AR 141. It rests on the western edge of Crowley's Ridge, which is a picturesque 100- to 200-foot-high geological phenomenon

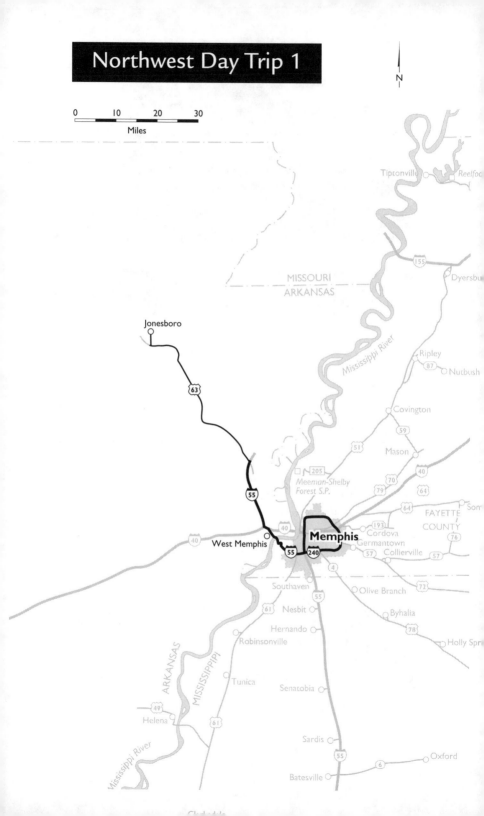

Northwest Day Trip 1

N

0   10   20   30
Miles

Tiptonville   Reelfoo

155
Dyersbu

MISSOURI
ARKANSAS

Jonesboro

63

Mississippi River

Ripley
87   Nutbush

Covington

59

51   Mason

205
Meeman-Shelby
Forest S.P.   70   40
79   64

55   64   FAYETTE
193   Cordova   COUNTY   Son
Memphis   Germantown   76
40   240   57   Collierville   57
West Memphis   55
4

Southaven   72
55
61   Nesbit   Byhalia

Hernando   78

Robinsonville   Holly Spri

ARKANSAS
MISSISSIPPI
Tunica

Senatobia

49
Helena   61

Sardis
55   Oxford

6

Mississippi River   Batesville

stretching across parts of Missouri and down to Helena, Arkansas, where it meets the Mississippi River. The park's lake offers year-round fishing; in fact, many consider Frierson one of the best fishing spots in Arkansas. If you show up in spring, you'll see the park's famous dogwoods dotting the landscape: Frierson claims to have more dogwoods than any other state park its size in Arkansas. The lake itself is 335 acres and home to a variety of fish: bass, bream, crappies, and catfish. The facilities include a visitor center, campsites, picnic areas with grills and tables, public rest rooms, a self-guided walking trail, playground, boat-launch ramp, and fishing pier. (870) 932-2615.

Arkansas State University Museum. 110 Cooley Drive, Jonesboro, AR 72467. The ASU Museum is housed in the west wing of Ellis Library; just look for the plesiosaur (sea monster–dinosaur) replica out front. Its exhibits, in addition to a general collection, focus on the natural and cultural history of Arkansas, including the time before its statehood. The permanent collection offers a look inside Arkansas's military, Native American, and natural history, among other world histories. Temporary exhibits likewise highlight Arkansas experience—for example, *Crowley's Ridge Parkway, a National Scenic Byway; The Path of Least Resistance: Transportation in Arkansas 1800-2000;* and, on a more literary note, *Picturing Hemingway: A Writer in His Time.* Anyone with an interest in Arkansas or the Midsouth should stop in to learn about the rich history of the state and region. Open daily except during university holidays. museum.astate.edu. (870) 972-2074.

The Fowler Center of Arkansas State University. 201 Olympic Drive, Jonesboro, AR 72467. If you can plan your trip to coincide with a concert sponsored by the Fowler Center, you'll be in for a real treat. Bands like the Glenn Miller Orchestra and the River City Brass Band, both nationally acclaimed, have played live for the crowds at the center. Call ahead for scheduled concerts or check out the ASU Web site: www.astate.edu. (870) 972-ASU1.

WHERE TO EAT

Demo's Barbecue & Smokehouse. 1851 South Church Street, Jonesboro, AR 72401. Demo's offers good, solid barbecue cooking. They smoke their own pigs; a full rack of ribs goes for less than $15.

You'll also find sandwiches and pork plates. $-$$; ☐. (870) 935-6633.

WHERE TO STAY

West Washington Guest House, Bed and Breakfast. 534 West Washington Avenue, Jonesboro, AR 72401. West Washington is a turn-of-the-twentieth-century, four-square building, and its owners boast a "relaxed, inviting atmosphere." Among the twelve guest rooms, each decorated in its own unique style and named for a famous Arkansan, is a suite complete with a whirlpool tub and sitting area. All of the beds are queens and all of the rooms have private bath. For community activities like cards, board games, and socializing, there's a sitting room and porch from which you can watch the hustle and bustle of the West Washington Avenue Historic District. Each morning, guests join one another in the dining room for a buffet breakfast, including a hot dish, pastries, fruit, and beverages. Drinks and snacks during the afternoon are also complimentary. $$-$$$; ☐. (870) 935-9300.

Regional Information

NORTH DAY TRIP 1

Tipton County Chamber of Commerce. 622 South Main Street, Covington, TN 38019. (901) 476-9727.

Nutbush/Tina Turner Heritage Center. (731) 772-4265.

Lauderdale County Chamber of Commerce. 103 East Jackson Street, Ripley, TN 38063. (901) 635-9541.

Dyer County Chamber of Commerce. 2000 Commerce Avenue, Dyersburg, TN 38024. (731) 285-3433.

NORTH DAY TRIP 2

Millington Chamber of Commerce. 7743 Church Street, Millington, TN 38053. (901) 872-1486.

NORTH DAY TRIP 3

Obion County Chamber of Commerce. 214 East Church Street, Union City, TN 38261. (901) 885-0211.

NORTHEAST DAY TRIP 1

Jackson Area Chamber of Commerce. 197 Auditorium Street, Jackson, TN 38301. (901) 423-2200.

Chamber of Commerce. 130 Main Street, Henderson, TN 37213. (731) 989-5222.

NORTHEAST DAY TRIP 2

Henry County Chamber of Commerce. 2508 East Wood Street, Paris, TN 38242. (731) 642-3431.

EAST

EAST DAY TRIP 1

Germantown Chamber of Commerce. 2195 Germantown Road South, Germantown, TN 38138. (901) 755-1200.

Collierville Chamber of Commerce. 215 South Center Street, Collierville, TN 38017. (901) 853-1949.

EAST DAY TRIP 2

Corinth Area Tourism and Promotion Council. 602 East Waldron Street, Corinth, MS 38834. (662) 287-8300; (800) 748-9048.

EAST DAY TRIP 3

Hardin County Tourism Board. 507 Main Street, Savannah, TN 38372. (731) 925-2364; (800) 552-FUNN.

EAST DAY TRIP 4

Fayette County Chamber of Commerce. 107 West Court Square, Somerville, TN 38068. (901) 465-8690.

SOUTHEAST

SOUTHEAST DAY TRIP 1

Holly Springs Chamber of Commerce. 154 South Memphis Street, Holly Springs, MS 38635. (662) 252-2943.

SOUTHEAST DAY TRIP 2

Tupelo Convention and Visitors Bureau. 399 East Main Street, Tupelo, MS 38804. (662) 841-6521; (800) 533-0611.

SOUTH

SOUTH DAY TRIP 1

Southaven Chamber of Commerce. 8700 Northwest Drive, Southaven, MS 36871. (662) 342-6365.

Olive Branch Chamber of Commerce. 6820 Cockrum Street, Olive Branch, MS 38654. (662) 895-2600.

SOUTH DAY TRIP 2

Sardis Chamber of Commerce. 114 West Lee Street, Sardis, MS 38666. (662) 487-3451.

SOUTH DAY TRIP 3

Oxford Tourism Council. 111 Courthouse Square, Oxford, MS 38655. (662) 234-4680; (800) 758-9177.

SOUTH DAY TRIP 4

Grenada Tourism Commission. 1321 Sunset Drive, Grenada, MS 38901. (662) 226-2571.

SOUTHWEST

SOUTHWEST DAY TRIP 1

Tunica Chamber of Commerce. 1371 P.O. Box 1888, Tunica, MS 38676. (662) 363-2865.

SOUTHWEST DAY TRIP 3

Helena Chamber of Commerce. 111 Hickory Hills Drive, Helena, AR 72342. (870) 838-8327.

WEST

WEST DAY TRIP 1

Memphis Convention and Visitors Bureau. 47 Union Avenue, Memphis, TN 38103. (901) 543-5300.

WEST DAY TRIP 2

West Memphis Chamber of Commerce. 108 West Broadway Street, West Memphis, AR 72310. (501) 735-1134.

WEST DAY TRIP 3

Little Rock Convention and Visitors Bureau. Robinson Center at Markham and Broadway, Little Rock, AR 72201. (501) 376-4781; (800) 844-4781.

WEST DAY TRIP 4

Pine Bluff Convention & Visitors Bureau. 1 Convention Center Plaza, Pine Bluff, AR 71601. (870) 536-7600.

NORTHWEST

NORTHWEST DAY TRIP 1

Greater Jonesboro Chamber of Commerce. 1709 East Nettleton, Jonesboro, AR 72403. (870) 932-6691.

Festivals and Celebrations

The multitude of special events and festivals throughout Tennessee, Mississippi, and Arkansas are a great testament to how much midsoutherners love to celebrate their land and their heritage. Any given month, you'll find cities hosting everything from tomato fests to Civil War commemorations. Most of the events are free and open to the public.

The Tennessee Tourist Development office can send you list of events in Tennessee. Write to 320 Sixth Avenue North, Rachel Jackson Building, Nashville, Tennessee 37243, or call (615) 741-2158 or (615) 741-2159. For a calendar of events in Arkansas, write to the Arkansas Department of Parks and Tourism, 1 Capital Mall, Little Rock, Arkansas 72201; call (800) NATURAL; or visit www.arkansas.com/. Information about Mississippi's events can be obtained from the Mississippi Division of Tourism, P.O. Box 849, Jackson, Mississippi 39205; (800) 927-6378; www.visitmississippi.org/.

In following list, you'll find the names of the various special events, listed in chronological order, along with their locations. For more information and descriptions of the events, please refer to the Special Events section in each day trip throughout the book.

MARCH

Women's NAIA Basketball Championships. Jackson, Tennessee.

Taste of Jackson. Jackson, Tennessee.

APRIL

Dogwood Festival and Dogwood Dash. Dyersburg, Tennessee.

World's Biggest Fish Fry. Paris, Tennessee.

Civil War reenactments. Shiloh, Tennessee.

Anniversary of the Battle of Shiloh. Shiloh, Tennessee.

Holly Springs Pilgrimage. Holly Springs, Mississippi.

Aberdeen Spring Pilgrimage. Aberdeen, Mississippi.

Springfest. Southaven, Mississippi.

Double-decker Festival. Oxford, Mississippi.

Tunica Rivergate Festival. Tunica, Mississippi.

Wild Hog Music Festival and Motorcycle Rally. Helena, Arkansas.

MAY

MidSouth Airshow. Millington, Tennessee.

Junior Fishing Rodeo. Meeman-Shelby Forest State Park, Tennessee.

The Jimmy Dean Foods Barbecue Festival. Dyersburg, Tennessee.

Spring Concert Series. Olive Branch, Mississippi.

May-Fest. Olive Branch, Mississippi.

Lofton Archery Classic and U.S. Championship. Grenada, Mississippi.

Wine, Food, and Art Extravaganza. Hot Springs, Arkansas.

Taste of Downtown Festival. Hot Springs, Arkansas.

Shannon Street Blues and Heritage Festival. Jackson, Tennessee.

Forked Deer Festival. Jackson, Tennessee.

Fair on the Square. Collierville, Tennessee.

JUNE

Frazier Park Fun Festival. Covington, Tennessee.

Summerfest. Meeman-Shelby Forest State Park, Tennessee.

Germantown Charity Horse Show. Germantown, Tennessee.

Sunset on the Square. Collierville, Tennessee.

The Elvis Presley Festival. Tupelo, Mississippi.

FedEx–St. Jude Classic Golf Tournament. (summer) Germantown, Tennessee.

Old Tyme Festival. Olive Branch, Mississippi.

Hot Springs Music Festival. Hot Springs, Arkansas.

JULY

Tomato Festival. Ripley, Tennessee.

Flag Day Celebration. Millington, Tennessee.

West Tennessee State Fair. Jackson, Tennessee.

Freedom Festival. Paris, Tennessee.

Fourth of July Family Celebration. Germantown, Tennessee.

Jacinto Fourth of July Festival. Corinth, Mississippi.

Slugburger Festival. Corinth, Mississippi.

Kudzu Festival. Holly Springs, Mississippi.

Wizard of Oz Children's Theatre Camp. Sardis, Mississippi.

AUGUST

Partners in Preservation. Collierville, Tennessee.

Union County Fair and Livestock Show. New Albany, Mississippi.

SEPTEMBER

Fall Concert Series. Olive Branch, Mississippi.

Hot Springs Street Art Festival. Hot Springs, Arkansas.

Hot Springs Jazz Festival. Hot Springs, Arkansas.

Arkansas Senior Olympic Games. Hot Springs, Arkansas.

Tipton County Fair and Heritage Day Festival. Covington, Tennessee.

Dyer County Fair. Dyersburg, Tennessee.

International Goat Days Family Festival. Millington, Tennessee.

Chickasaw Bluffs Appreciation Day. Meeman-Shelby Forest State Park, Tennessee.

Archeofest. Jackson, Tennessee.

Great Casey Jones Balloon Classic. Jackson, Tennessee.

Britton Lane Battle Reenactment. Jackson, Tennessee.

African Street Festival. Jackson, Tennessee.

Eiffel Tower Day. Paris, Tennessee.

Annual Storytelling Festival. Paris, Tennessee.

Germantown Festival. Germantown, Tennessee.

Hog Wild in Corinth Barbecue Festival. Corinth, Mississippi.

OCTOBER

Great Pumpkin Patch Halloween Festival. Covington, Tennessee.

Choctaw Indian Festival. Ripley, Tennessee.

McIvers Bluff Founders Day Festival. Dyersburg, Tennessee.

James Logan Colbert Living Day. Meeman-Shelby Forest State Park, Tennessee.

Architectural Treasures of Fayette County Tour. Fayette County, Tennessee.

White Oak Fall Festival. Byhalia, Mississippi.

Battle of Tupelo reenactment. Tupelo, Mississippi.

Blue Bluff River Festival. Aberdeen, Mississippi.

Octoberfest. Olive Branch, Mississippi.

Old Towne Street Rod Run. Olive Branch, Mississippi.

National Foxhunt Chase. Grenada, Mississippi.

Tunica Harvest Festival. Tunica, Mississippi.

King Biscuit Blues Festival. Helena, Arkansas.

Main Street Fall Festival and Chili Cook-Off. West Memphis, Tennessee.

Pine Bluff Film Festival. Pine Bluff, Arkansas.

Spa City Blues Festival. Hot Springs, Arkansas.

Hot Springs Documentary Film Festival. Hot Springs, Arkansas.

Arkansas Oktoberfest. Hot Springs, Arkansas.

NOVEMBER

Sportsfest. Hot Springs, Arkansas.

DECEMBER

Lambuth Area Neighborhood Association Holiday Fundraiser. Jackson, Tennessee.

Dickens on the Square. Collierville, Tennessee.

Santa Express. Collierville, Tennessee.

Southern Lights. Southaven, Mississippi.

Christmas in Dixie Tour of Antebellum Homes. Hernando, Mississippi.

West Memphis Dickens of a Christmas. West Memphis, Arkansas.

State Parks

There are more than fifty state parks in the Tennessee state park system, each offering a unique and exciting array of activities. Excellent hiking trails can be found in Meeman-Shelby State Park, Chickasaw State Park, and Pinson Mounds State Park. If you're interested in playing a round of golf, choose from T. O. Fuller State Park or Pickwick Landing State Park. For bird-watching and fishing, don't miss Reelfoot Lake.

Most of Tennessee's state parks feature campgrounds, and a few have cabins and inns to select from. All state parks offer a variety of outdoor activities. Keep in mind that Tennessee law requires hunters and anglers to be licensed, so check into the state regulations before taking part in these activities. For more information, contact the Tennessee Wildlife Resources Agency, P.O. Box 40747, Nashville, TN 37204; (615) 781-6622.

To learn about the multitude of special events hosted throughout the parks of Tennessee, contact Program Services division of the Tennessee state parks system by calling (615) 532-0016. And to get more information about Tennessee parks themselves, you can write Tennessee State Parks, 401 Church Street, Nashville, TN 37243; (800) 421-6683. You can also visit them on the Web by logging on to www.tnstateparks.com.

Mississippi boasts twenty-eight state parks within its borders and offers some of the best hunting in the United States. Hunters will find approximately 800,000 acres of game habitat in thirty-eight wildlife management areas. Many of these sites can be found within this book. The Mississippi state park system takes great pride in offering unspoiled woodlands, fields, and marshes filled with a wide variety of game.

Fishing is by far one of the most popular ways to spend free time among visitors to Mississippi's parks. The mild climate of the area allows fish a year-round growing season—and also encourages anglers to cast their lines almost any time of the year. The Mississippi Department of Wildlife, Fisheries and Parks oversees twenty-one lakes within the park system, including Sardis Lake and Grenada Lake. To obtain a license (using a credit card) through the Mississippi Department of Wildlife, Fisheries and Parks, call (800) 5GO–HUNT.

For more information about the Mississippi state park system, contact the Mississippi Department of Wildlife, Fisheries and Parks at 1505 Eastover Drive, Jackson, MS 39211; (662) 432–2400; www.mdwfp.com.

ARKANSAS

Arkansas's fifty-one state parks offer lodges, cabins, and riverside campsites, not to mention prehistoric Indian mounds. One of the most popular is Hot Springs National Park, known for its natural hot-water geysers. And the Ozark Mountains provide a gorgeous backdrop for a variety of hiking trails within the state's parks. Don't miss the fun events and activities held throughout the year at many of the parks in Arkansas.

For the adventurous, there's Crater of Diamonds Park in Murfreesboro, where visitors can search for and keep real diamonds throughout a thirty-six-acre field, which is the location of an ancient, gem-bearing volcanic pipe in the earth's surface.

To find out more about Arkansas's state parks, contact the Arkansas Department of Parks and Tourism, 1 Capitol Mall, Little Rock, AR 72201; (888) AT–PARKS; www.arkansasstateparks.com.

Midsouthern Heritage

When you think about the Midsouth, a number of different land-marks come to mind—the Mississippi River, the Ozark Mountains, the Delta bluffs. And it's hard to imagine what life was like before the casinos in Tunica or the myriad ethnic restaurants in downtown Memphis. But centuries of civilizations have intertwined to give us our heritage.

The most primitive ancestors in our area date back to the prehis-toric period. During this time, a number of Native American tribes ruled the land, ranging from hunters and gatherers to mound builders. Around the 1500s tribes such as the Chickasaw, Yuchi, Cherokee, Choctaw, Natchez dominated the areas we know today as Tennessee, Mississippi, Arkansas, and parts of Alabama. Over time the Cherokee and Chickasaw tribes grew to dominate most of Tennessee. One of the first Europeans to come in contact with these two tribes was the Spanish explorer and conquistador Hernando de Soto. In 1541 he set up camp near what is now Memphis. Because this was the first exposure the Native Americans had to Europeans, they had no immunity built up to the diseases the white people brought with them. Over the next decade, the Indian population dramatically dropped throughout the Midsouth. De Soto and his men scavenged the area around Arkansas looking for gold and silver; it's believed that de Soto died in the territory of Arkansas.

Following the Spanish came the French. By the time French explorers reached the Mississippi Valley area, almost all the land was uninhabited. Tribes such as the Quapaw lived along the Arkansas River and near the Mississippi River. Explorers such as Jacques Marquette and Louis Joliet and Rene-Robert Cavelier traded along these rivers. Pierre le Moyne led the way in building a number of French forts throughout the Gulf Coast around what is now Ocean Springs and Biloxi. By 1717 Scottish financier John Law had become an influential man in the French court through his financial interest in the French bank. He led the way in encouraging immigrants to settle in the area along the Gulf Coast and participate in mining and trading.

By the late seventeenth century, the English had begun to set up forts around the Midsouth as well, and wars began to break about between the English and French, with a variety of Indian tribes choosing sides. During the 1800s, towns such as Little Rock and Jackson came into existence. The Choctaw and Chickasaw tribes ceded their land to the federal government and agreed to move out of their former home. This move brought settlers by the droves to the area around the Mississippi River. By the mid-1800s the population of Mississippi had shot up to almost 800,000. Forty-five percent of the inhabitants were white, with the majority of the population being African American slaves brought to the area to pick cotton, the foremost means of income for the area. Towns along the Mississippi River provided fertile land for agriculture, as well as port destinations for ships carrying cargo. In fact, Memphis is still known as the nation's Distribution Capital.

This boom in cotton growth caused plantation owners to see slavery as a necessity, allowing them to keep their respective states profitable. It was this mind-set that encouraged southerners to secede from the rest of the United States during the Civil War. During this time, slaves and freedmen alike struggled to extract friends and family members from plantations to the urban areas of the northern United States via the Underground Railroad. This famous passageway is brought to life through the tours of some of its former stopping points, including a plantation known as Slavehaven in northern Memphis.

After the Civil War slavery was abolished, yet much of the South remained segregated. The outcome of the war could not make people join together as one. Organizations such as the Congress of Racial Equality, the Student Nonviolent Coordinating Committee, and the National Association for the Advancement of Colored People banded together to make their presence known. And the 1954 decision of the U.S. Supreme Court in *Brown v. Board of Education* put an end to segregation in schools once and for all.

In the meantime, the cropping of cotton had begun to decrease. In its place, other forms of farming had to be found. Tyson Foods led the way in chicken farming; Sam Walton spurred the growth of his famous Wal-Mart stores throughout Arkansas. And during this time, a new group of people was emerging. Throughout the Midsouth, the Hispanic population has risen dramatically over the past several decades.

Today the Midsouth is a hodgepodge of inhabitants, each with a unique heritage. We come from Africa, Europe, Mexico, and Asia, but we all combine to form the South—ancestors of farm migrants and slaves alongside descendants of wealthy European barons. Once a racially divided section of the United States, the New South is emerging as a more tolerant place for children to be reared. Programs such as Love Thy Neighbor in Memphis are bringing together people from all socioeconomic and racial backgrounds to show that together, we can build a better future. The National Civil Rights Museum serves as a reminder that, as we move forward, we must never forget our past.